Living Calm

PATRICIA HOFER

patricia@yieldingtochristianity.com

www.yieldingtochristianity.com

Living Calm

Published by Wheatmark®
1760 East River Road, Suite 145
Tucson, Arizona 85718 USA
www.wheatmark.com

ISBN: 978-1-62787-362-8 (paperback)
ISBN: 978-1-62787-363-5 (ebook)
LCCN: 2015957934

Thank you, Ted, for taking the lovely pictures
and drawing me into travel,
for proofreading every word of every book,
and for applying your eye for logic
to what appeared to you at times as an illogical journey.

Introduction

OUR SLOW GLIDE ALONG the Yangtze introduced us to a culture that continuously nurtures the lives of millions of determined and marvelously creative people. The quadrangle homes, which form the alleys or hutongs of Beijing, sheltered the resilient generations of proud families. Their strength and scope of purpose evidenced itself from the Great Wall to the terra cotta warriors, from Tiananmen Square to the ancient Zeng Houyi chimes in Shanghai, ringing out a melody with notes created 2,500 years ago!

But the marvelous mystery of silk weaving is perhaps my most enduring image of the Chinese people. The small silk rug hanging on my living room wall immediately brings to my mind their appreciation of beauty and order and innovation.

This softly pliable silk rug, which would have taken one person many years to weave, is as delicately lovely on the back as it is on the front. As I walk around the room, the subtly changing colors of the threads offer hints of the living thing that they emerged from. A silk rug of this quality needs to have at least 1,000 knots per square inch. In order to count them, I had to learn that one little knot looks like two dots paired together.

For me, these patiently woven, silken knots have now become a metaphor for the varying moments of my life, the times and events that flow together to form a tapestry of who I am and what I believe. And, since childhood, some of my brightest and most inspiring thoughts have emerged from Christian hymns and poems. Their internal melodies and rhyming syllables have created beautiful "knots" of comfort, delivering me from fear and sadness, overflowing my heart with joy.

So in this book, which is the last of a series, these bright weavings of inspiration are my focus. Whether we realize it or not, whether we embrace it or not, we all live in God's eternity. And His Christ is the warp and woof of our unique individuality, the fabric of each human soul.

Please, Lord,

Hold me in this calm, secret place,
Confident, quiet, and free.
Circled around by your embrace
Where there's only you and me.

Cleanse my sad heart with your spirit;
Light it, fill it with your peace.
So when you speak, I can hear it—
Selfish distractions all cease.

Free my weary soul from worry,
Help me feel you by my side.
Shelter me from stress and hurry,
Loving Saviour, strength and guide.

Relieve my mind from managing
The tasks I must or would do.
Turn stubborn will into yielding
To wonder that comes from you.

Show me my eternal calling.
Pour it over me anew,
The grace that keeps me from falling,
The restful Spirit that's you.

Take this, my plea, as your token,
Refine it, make it be true.
A vow that cannot be broken,
A life lived always with you.

Patricia Hofer (2015)

Day by Day Verses

I Need Thee Every Hour (Annie Hawks 1872)

1. Only Christ's presence
2. The temptation of certitude
3. His rich promises

My Saviour (Patricia Hofer 2005)

4. Singleness of focus
5. Christ healing
6. Moments of eternity
7. The secret of self-abandonment
8. Our larger life

In Heavenly Love Abiding (Anna Letitia Waring 1850)

9. Always home
10. Beside you now
11. Not self-dependent and alone

Larger than… (Patricia Hofer 2013)

12. Living in abundance
13. Living in eternity
14. Living with abandon
15. Living with companionship
16. Living in his vibrant life

Give us day by day our daily bread (Josiah Conder 1836)

17. Today's lessons
18. Foreboding fears
19. Sanguine hopes
20. Inspired moments

Sanctifying Grace (Patricia Hofer 2011)

21. Make me better
22. A special plan for each of us
23. Less is more
24. St. Patrick's simple truths
25. Our human concerns
26. Our second blessing

Dear Lord and Father of mankind (John Greenleaf Whittier 1872)

27. Foolish ways
28. Simple trust
29. Strain and stress
30. The gentle whisper of calm

Christ, whose glory fills the skies (Charles Wesley 1740)

31. A light shining in a dark place
32. Comforter and Companion
33. The perfect day

More than what we seem (Patricia Hofer 2009)

34. Wondering and worshipping
35. Our living soul
36. Saviour and Friend
37. The higher goal
38. Our humanity

39. The home of His heart
40. The larger, stronger, calmer life

Here O my Lord (Horatius Bonar 1855)
41. Face to face
42. Hallowed moments
43. Drinking the cup
44. As basic as bread

Our Strength (Patricia Hofer 2014)
45. Unique and ageless
46. Living beyond the brick wall
47. Testing our thoughts
48. Within us and with us
49. Pushing back despair
50. Born from above

Still, still with Thee (Harriet Beecher Stowe 1855)
51. Fairer than morning
52. Alone with Him
53. The Lord's new morning
54. The sweetness of sleep
55. Just another sunrise

Please Lord (Patricia Hofer 2015)
56. Circled around
57. Heart changes
58. The burden inside
59. Relief
60. Down there with the Lord
61. Power of yielding

1

I need thee every hour,
most gracious Lord;
no tender voice like thine
can peace afford.

Annie Hawks (1872)

THE THINGS THAT WAKE us up to our need for God are not always obvious—but fear is often involved. We may be afraid of dying or losing a loved one. Or we may see our security slipping away with the loss of a job or a home. Whatever the need appears to be on the outside, what we really need on the inside is God. That was true for me, particularly, when I feared abandonment.

For almost two decades, I'd been haunted by a recurring dream that I would once again be alone. And my first husband did drive off one day, leaving me in a large city with a low-paying job—far from friends or family. Interestingly, when that happened, the reality of actually being abandoned made the dream stop. It was unnecessary, I guess.

I think the disciples worried about abandonment as well. They couldn't imagine life without their friend and teacher, their messiah. And yet, Jesus was telling them that he was going to "go away," going to be "leaving the world" (John 14:28; 16:28). He also told them something else they likely didn't understand—that it would be to their "advantage" when that happened (NASB 16:7). And yet, what they learned after Christ's resurrection and ascension, after the return of Jesus' Spirit at Pentecost, was that it *was* to their advantage. In that way, the Lord would always be present with them, wherever they went.

And Christ is always present with us as well. During my lonely time, it wasn't Bible reading or doctrinal believing or some supportive prayer group that pushed back my fear and isolation. My one enduring comfort and peace was the Lord himself, his companioning presence. And so most mornings since that time I sing along with Annie Hawks:

> I need thee, O I need thee,
> every hour I need thee!
> O bless me now, my Savior—
> I come to thee.

2

I need thee every hour;
stay thou near by;
temptations lose their power
when thou art nigh.

Annie Hawks (1872)

TEMPTATIONS WOULD BE EASIER to recognize if they all were as obviously ugly and off putting as Tolkien's orcs and trolls. But they aren't. Sometimes I don't even realize that I'm being tempted down the wrong road until I'm stubbornly committed to it, totally lost in the certitude of knowing that I know.

Perhaps that's why C. S. Lewis concluded that it's not the physical sins but the spiritual sins that are the worst (*Mere Christianity*, "Sexual Morality"). Rooted in our heart rather than in our body, stubborn certitude is indeed a spiritual sin. Being proud of being right tempts us in ways that can damage all areas of our lives—our family relationships and friendships, our careers, and our neighborliness.

And when this proud certitude finds its way into our Christian believing, we're truly lost. It is self-righteousness that tempts us into thinking we have the truth and others do not. Enthralled in the pride of our own believing, we might even be tempted to turn spiritual experience into some kind of a competition. Left unchecked, this spiritual pride builds a faith in ourselves that could eventually diminish or replace our faith in God.

And yet, our relationship with God isn't based on being perfectly righteous or having a firm grasp on doctrinal truth or moral certitude. As Jesus says, God's kingdom is for those who "change and become like little children" (NIV Matt. 18:3). For sinful temptations to lose their power, we must lose our power. And so each morning I continue to sing along with Annie's refrain:

> I need thee, O I need thee,
> every hour I need thee!
> O bless me now, my Savior—
> I come to thee.

3

I need thee every hour,
teach me thy will;
and thy rich promises
in me fulfill.

Annie Hawks (1872)

How God's "RICH PROMISES" are going to play out in our lives can be confusing. At least that is what I've experienced after my remarkable saving moment with the Lord. At first, I just kind of drifted along blissfully, feeling so comforted, so blessed. And yet, even while I was moving back to Arizona and working into a different job, the questions started coming, "Why me, Lord. Why did this happen to me?"

My search for answers led me to start reading. One inspired Christian writer after another took me by the hand. C. S. Lewis' *Mere Christianity* introduced me to a lifetime of thoughts. And then one day during those years, I was walking near my house in Glendale, feeling reassured by the beautiful experience Charles Raven shared in his book *A Wanderer's Way* (1929). That was the moment when the thought finally slipped in that maybe I was supposed to write something too. And yet, at the time, I had no idea what I would say or how I would even begin.

Hawks' inspired line, "teach me thy will," surprised me with insight. It was not *my* "will" and *my* "rich promises" but God's. He does the creating of purpose and He does the fulfilling. And that is true for all of us. The role we play, the only role we can play, is the yielding. So every day, you and I both need to sing along with Annie:

I need thee, O I need thee,
every hour I need thee!
O bless me now, my Savior—
I come to thee.

I need thee every hour,
most gracious Lord;
no tender voice like thine
can peace afford.

Refrain:
I need thee, O I need thee,
every hour I need thee!
O bless me now, my Savior--
I come to thee!

I need thee every hour;
stay thou near by;
temptations lose their power
when thou art nigh. [Refrain]

I need thee every hour;
teach me thy will,
and thy rich promises
in me fulfill. [Refrain]

I need thee every hour,
Most Holy One;
O make me thine indeed,
thou blessed Son.

Annie Hawks (1872)

4

Tender Christ, forever near,
Help me feel your presence here.
Focus me on thy pure light,
Inward singleness of sight.

THIS FIRST POEM CAME to me as I began realizing that walking with the living Savior wasn't something that I had to do or get done. He was going to be the doer, the one who got things done! That change of perspective has freed me in so many ways.

For example, have you ever tried to pray and just couldn't make the thoughts connect? Or maybe you were too distracted and your mind kept wandering off? This struggle between praying and distraction is not unlike Jesus' references to a "kingdom" or "house" that is "divided against itself" (NIV Mark 3:24). Two things are always feuding in our mental "house."

Today, now that research can more clearly distinguish brain function from consciousness, the word *focus* takes on new meaning. The brain focuses on mundane, earthbound needs and wants—what we're having for breakfast or how we'll pay our bills. And yet, at the very same time, our consciousness aspires to something higher—Christly love and forgiveness, compassion and kindness.

When we are distracted, we are, in many ways, divided against ourselves, just as Jesus is describing. But then Jesus follows with this: "In fact, no one can enter a strong man's house without first tying him up. Then he can plunder the strong man's house" (NIV Mark 3:27).

The brain with its natural desires and instincts is clearly, for me, the "strong man." Our problem is that we alone can't "bind" it or tie it up. But Christ, the living Saviour, can and does do that. And so sometimes the need for us is to sit still and be quiet, allowing the pure and tender light of Christ to flood our consciousness with the "singleness" of his focus.

5

Healing Christ, deliver me.
Spirit whole and sound and free
Deep within my heart abide;
Loose my soul of pain and pride.

CONTRARY TO WHAT WE may sometimes hear, God's intention is not illness. Being sick is never His punishment. Even when we know that we've violated some health or safety precaution, we aren't out of the reach of God's law of love and forgiveness. The living Saviour is always right here, walking with us and reassuring us of that fact.

That's why the many Christ healings we encounter in the Gospels are such a great comfort. Once on the Sabbath, Jesus "loosed" a woman, freeing her from a crippling condition that she'd had for eighteen years. Instead of rejoicing as they should have been doing, those around him in the synagogue took pride in criticizing Jesus for violating the Sabbath (Luke 13:10-17).

And still today, contrary to what anyone else might think, Christ is always abiding in our heart and by our side, always waiting to "loose" us, to free us and heal us in ways that only he is able to do. So we don't ever need to walk into a doctor's office or a surgery alone. We don't ever need to face the adversity of chronic illness by ourselves. The living Saviour, our advocate and comforter, is walking with us, waiting for us to put our hand in his.

When we abandon our doubts to him, the Lord delivers us from these uncertainties, flooding our consciousness with assurance and renewed faith. When we stop trying to carry the burden of responsibility ourselves, the Lord delivers us with his sustaining strength, moving the load from our shoulder to his. When, at last, we yield, the Lord delivers us with his comforting presence. Wrapping his love around us, he replaces our loneliness and despair with companionship. As Jesus says in John, "My Father is always working, and so am I" (NLT John 5:17).

6

Joyous Christ, sweet inner glow,
Oh that you can move me so,
Trade thou darkest night for peace—
Daunting fears for glad release.

THE POPULAR PHRASE "HAVING a moment" describes our desire to experience the depth and significance of life, to be moved by the meaning in what goes on around us. And so we stand quietly, drinking in the shared love of a family gathering. We stare transfixed, trying to make a permanent imprint of a ruggedly beautiful mountain pass or the depths of the Grand Canyon. We replay again and again some moving melody that stirs our spirit, trying to forever weave it into our soul.

But even these things fade in the constantly changing seconds of passing time. They don't give us, in any permanent way, the harmony and joy of soul that we are thirsting for. What we need to recognize is that this yearning for "a moment" is not a natural one but a spiritual one. Misunderstanding this is similar to the Samaritan woman's mistake at Jacob's well. At first, she thought Jesus was promising magic, a single drink of water that would miraculously cure her of thirst (John 4:15). For someone who had to walk a distance to get water, that probably did sound really attractive.

But "the gift of God" that Jesus was offering the woman was not the water of natural experience but Christ's living revitalizing presence. He was offering the living joy and assurance that would forever continue, "a spring of water welling up to eternal life" (NIV John 4:10, 14).

And my experience is that the Lord still does that. He's still offering each of us, day by day, the "living water" that renews us and satisfies us. When we open ourselves to him, the inflowing of Christ's life and the glow of his love moves us in unimaginable ways. We experience "a moment" that overflows into eternity.

7

Loving Christ, eternal friend,
On thee only I depend.
Make my life serene and still
With the sureness of thy will.

AN OLD HYMN THAT I grew up with, one by William F. Sherwin, asked, "Why is thy faith, O child of God, so small?" And that question still comes to my mind sometimes. The difference now, after my time with the Lord, is that I have an answer that is actually helpful.

Our faith in God is "so small" because our faith in ourselves is so big! Before my life crashed and burned in my 30's, I suffered badly from this wrong kind of faith—faith in myself. Religious fervor draws some people more than others. And I was a lost cause. If you had been there to witness my religious zeal with my proud-willed surety that I could pray my way out of anything, you'd get the idea. Years of failure did eventually humble some of that certitude out of me.

And now, my walk with the Lord has continued the process. Religious faith, as I now experience it, isn't simply a positive attitude, a way of getting the things I'm just sure

God wants me to have. And faith also isn't about strength of will, willing ourselves into wellness—or success or happiness. Faith in God is faith *in God*—not faith *in our ability* to be deserving or devoted or steadfast.

So, if we really want to enlarge our faith, the place to begin is to take small steps into self-abandonment. Sometimes that can mean being less determined and controlling in managing our possessions or our money or our relationships. At other times it might be offering fewer opinions and less advice.

And, probably most helpful of all, we need to meekly abandon our ideas of how things must work out. We need to stop trying to control what will happen. And so, no matter what the concern, we pray, "Here it is, Lord. You take it." We are Christ's and Christ is Lord of all. We're safe with him, regardless of the outcome.

8

Saving Christ, be thou my mind,
All compassionate and kind.
Open self that I might see
Without you there is no me.

WHEN I WROTE THIS poem over fifteen years ago, the sentences started coming while I was exercising. And when I was finished, I sat down and wrote out the poem. At the time, I didn't really even understand this last verse all that well myself. The last line was even a bit startling to me.

But many years of research and reading and praying has made its meaning clearer. Support for it can be found in the writings of St. Paul where he says, "But we have the mind of Christ" (1 Cor. 2:16). And Colossians tells us Christ "was there before anything was made, and all things continue because of him" (NCV 1:17).

What I now see, and have found immensely helpful, is that our higher consciousness is God-derived, something human beings receive with the Creator's "breath of life." The subjectivity and individuality we have, our ability to step back and look at ourselves, isn't present anywhere else but in each of us.

To "open self" is to open our heart and mind, to step back and recognize when we're being dragged down into selfish, brain-centered responses. Then, when our thinking is flooded with fear of illness, we pray to the Lord, "be thou my mind." When we can't sleep because of worry, we reach out to the Saviour saying, "be thou my mind." When we have been imposed on and want to strike back, we ask for Christ's help saying, "be thou my mind.

The same Christ that was present at the moment of our creation is with us now — "all things continue because of him." He, and not the natural world, is the source of our conscious individuality, the larger life that we human beings all have.

My Saviour

Tender Christ, forever near,
Help me feel your presence here.
Focus me on thy pure light,
Inward singleness of sight.

Healing Christ, deliver me.
Spirit whole and sound and free
Deep within my heart abide;
Loose my soul of pain and pride.

Joyous Christ, sweet inner glow,
Oh that you can move me so,
Trade thou darkest night for peace—
Daunting fears for glad release.

Loving Christ, eternal friend,
On thee only I depend.
Make my life serene and still
With the sureness of thy will.

Saving Christ, be thou my mind,
All compassionate and kind.
Open self that I might see
Without you there is no me.

Patricia Hofer (2005)

9

In heavenly love abiding,
no change my heart shall fear.
And safe in such confiding,
for nothing changes here.
The storm may roar without me,
my heart may low be laid,
But God is round about me,
and can I be dismayed?

Anna Laetitia Waring (1850)

BUT OF COURSE WE do fear change, particularly the changes we can't control. And sometimes those changes have something to do with distance. Whether we're moving across town or across the country or to another country, change is a scary thing.

Because Anna Waring is a 19th century writer, I tend to think that she is probably using "without" as a place, as in outside somewhere. But for me, "without" means that I'm going to let the storm do its thing *without* me, *without* my participation, *without* my involvement. As I've often described it, I'm going to step off the planet and let it spin on *without* me!

Such a disconnection is possible as long as we know that "God is round about" us, regardless of where we are and no matter what kind of storm we're facing. Our presence with God and in God never changes. As the psalmist said, we might even "dwell in the uttermost parts of the sea" (Ps. 139:9). Even there or here or wherever, the Lord is guiding us and holding us close.

This absence of distance now helps me when Ted is off hiking in the Australian outback or the Himalayas or the Andes. But the idea has a long history with me. I needed Waring's inspired words as a young woman leaving home, moving from South Dakota to Arizona. And I desperately needed her comfort again when I was abandoned in Boston with really no one to blame but myself.

Since childhood, this hymn has reassured me that there is no distance in God's "heavenly love." When we live in the Lord's abiding presence, we're always home.

10

Wherever He may guide me,
no want shall turn me back.
My Shepherd is beside me,
and nothing can I lack.
His wisdom ever waking,
His sight is never dim.
He knows the way He's taking,
and I will walk with Him.

Anna Laetitia Waring (1850)

I'M NOW NOT SURE I was guided to Boston when I went to that second youth conference as a teen. Maybe I wasn't even guided to the first one a couple of years earlier. But I was back there again. This time a girlfriend from my Sunday school class went along.

When we arrived at the hotel where we had a reservation, we found it to be a disgusting, seedy mess. There was no way we felt safe there. Flimsy locks and thin walls. So we grabbed our stuff and moved to the dormitory where I'd stayed before. We weren't prepared for a dorm room, but some others there shared a couple of blankets and towels.

Anyway, I was lying on my top bunk clutching my one

blanket, exhausted and scared to death. And then the words of Waring's hymn came to me, and I went over them and over them again. The Shepherd is ever awake, she says, and "no want shall turn me back." Then I suddenly felt God's presence surrounding me. And that presence transformed the entryway light that we'd left on—making its globe enlarge and radiate with warmth and comfort and safety.

That night—when I was only a freshman in college and off on a willful trek that maybe shouldn't ever have happened—I felt surrounded by God's presence. And the image that brings that experience back with total clarity is the glow of that hallway light.

Over the intervening decades, the comforting awareness I experienced in that dorm room in Boston has never faded or dimmed. My Shepherd was beside me then and is beside me now. And that same living Saviour is beside you now as well.

11

Green pastures are before me,
which yet I have not seen.
Bright skies will soon be over me,
where darkest clouds have been.
My hope I cannot measure,
my path to life is free.
My Savior has my treasure,
and He will walk with me.

Anna Laetitia Waring (1850)

WARING'S NATURAL IMAGES OF "green pastures" and "bright skies" appealed to me a great deal when I was growing up. I trusted the idea that all of these blessings were before me, waiting to be experienced. But, as much as I liked visualizing the promise of these natural images in my youth, there came a time when they didn't help me that much.

When I was isolated, struggling alone and working in various jobs and large cities, the future didn't hold much hope. Sometimes I was digging into my small amount of savings just to pay monthly bills. Those times when I was struggling with the dark of depression, my habit was to say the words of this hymn, over and over in my mind. Eventually I saw past the bright promises to something else. And that's why, decades ago, and still today, the comfort I find in the third verse of Waring's poem comes in its last line—"and He will walk with me."

What this assurance gave me was the realization that God didn't just drop us into a bunch of moral and human struggles and then step back to watch how we handle them. We're not abandoned here, self-existent and alone, navigating our way through this world's obstacle course. As Jesus told his disciples in John, we aren't expected to bear fruit here by ourselves, an isolated branch separated from its vine, from its source (15:4).

The "treasure" Christ has for us is that we are always companioned, always walking with him, ever connected and loved and forgiven. What finally reversed my years of hardship and struggle was a new and growing relationship with "my Savior."

In heavenly love abiding, no change my heart shall fear.
And safe in such confiding, for nothing changes here.
The storm may roar without me, my heart may low be laid,
But God is round about me, and can I be dismayed?

Wherever He may guide me, no want shall turn me back.
My Shepherd is beside me, and nothing can I lack.
His wisdom ever waking, His sight is never dim.
He knows the way He's taking, and I will walk with Him.

Green pastures are before me, which yet I have not seen.
Bright skies will soon be over me, where darkest clouds have
    been.
My hope I cannot measure, my path to life is free.
My Savior has my treasure, and He will walk with me.

Anna Laetitia Waring (1850)

12

Larger than ever-spreading sky,
Stronger than ev'ry law of earth,
Calmer than a mirror-like sea,
Is the God-Life that gives you birth.

THIS VERSE WAS WRITTEN a couple of years before my husband and I visited the fiords in southern Chile. But I knew immediately that the picture of calm his picture captured was the image for the poem and also for this book's cover. The Chilean fiord was so beautiful, reflections everywhere, with barely a ripple!

But nature's "mirror-like sea" doesn't last. Even the next day there was windy turmoil as we took a boat tour up into the fiords and glaciers. But that's okay. Nature wasn't intended to be unchanging. Rather, it is to be a symbol, only a hint of who our Creator is. As Lewis wrote in *Mere Christianity*, "Everything God has made has some likeness to Himself." But the "greatness of space" is not the same as the greatness of God. The "hugeness" of the universe is only a "translation," Lewis wrote, "a sort of symbol" ("Making and Begetting").

Without the seeming limitlessness of the night sky and

the rhythms of the sun and the moon, for example, what would draw our gaze upward and stretch our soul? The very immensity of space is what gives us some understanding of the all-encompassing presence of a transcendent Creator.

Similarly, God's being, His Spirit of life, is greater than the teeming natural life we see here on earth. The Father-Creator, whom Jesus also calls "our Father," sent his Son to show us His vibrancy of life. Christ didn't need the resurrection to understand what this God-Life includes. But we human beings desperately did need it. As Jesus' promised, "I am come that they might have life, and that they might have it more abundantly" (KJ John 10:10). Oh, how I love the possibilities and the calm of our God-inspired, continuing life!

13

Larger than any span of time,
Stronger far than bone and sinew,
Calmer than nature's ebbing flow,
Is the God-Love that breathes in you.

As I WROTE IN the previous chapter, any calm in nature is usually deceiving. We have the calm before the storm and the calm after the storm but always and ever, the storm. Similarly, an ebbing tide could appear more peaceful, but that's really only because the tide is pulling away from us, receding instead of pushing toward us.

This word *ebbing* is also sometimes used to describe the wasting away or weakening of our physical existence. Sooner or later, each of us encounters the frail and temporary nature of our brains and bodies. And, like the tide, when our stamina and wellness start to recede, they appear to be diminishing.

When this started happening to me, I was tempted—and probably everyone is—to hold desperately to my evolutionary wisp of life, as fleeting and insubstantial as I knew it was. Some days I would frantically follow every health suggestion that appeared valid and do-able. Other days I'd start racing around, hoping to make every moment count. And then, too, there were the times I just wanted to stick my head in the sand, hoping to ignore what lay ahead.

After decades of struggle and striving with lack and illness, I finally just gave up. And at that moment, as amazing as it still is to me, the Lord was there, lifting me up and filling me with light and joy. And that's remained true ever since. His inspiration and healing calm happens when I quit trying, when I yield.

So, although I do make a few other points again and again in my writing, the purpose and power behind everything I write is this peaceful surety that comes with self-abandonment. Christ is stronger than "bone and sinew." Christ is "larger than any span of time." When we yield, when we abandon our own self-effort, we'll discover the calm of living with the Lord in eternity.

14

Living larger, stronger, calmer
Is what the Saviour comes to show
To his Father's loved and loving
Children who labor here below.

CHRISTIAN THEOLOGIANS HAVE SPENT centuries attempting to explain who Jesus Christ was and is. His salvation and sacrifice. His forgiveness and compassion. His continuing comfort and peace. And many theological doctrines can be helpful as ways for us to experience or to embrace what Christ taught.

But it's clear to me now, and has been ever since my conversion experience, that these joys of salvation are not things we can arrive at through self-effort. They are not personality changes we ourselves can initiate in any permanent way. And so, as Lewis wrote, we need to stand back each day from our "natural fussings and frettings." Abandoning our natural pride and self-centered focus, we can then begin "listening to that other voice, taking that other point of view, letting that other larger, stronger, quieter life come flowing in" (*Mere Christianity*, "Is Christianity Hard or Easy?").

What has helped me in this daily yielding is seeing how

often Jesus did it, how many times Christ stepped back, honoring his Father and diminishing himself. He says, for example, "the Son can do nothing by himself; he can do only what he sees his Father doing" (NIV John 5:19). And yet again Jesus says, "By myself I can do nothing; … for I seek not to please myself but him who sent me" (NIV John 5:30). And then, of course, at Gethsemane Jesus prays to his Father, saying, "not my will, but yours be done" (NIV Luke 22:42).

This self-abnegation that the Lord practiced towards his Father, so often and so effortlessly, is only possible for you and I now and then, one moment here, one moment there. But, because we are the Father's "loved and loving children," abandoning self-interest could occur more and more—if we'd let it. The question then becomes, how available to Christ's "larger, stronger, quieter life" are we going to allow ourselves to be?

15

Larger than all our loneliness,
Stronger than all our willful cries,
Calmer with each new forgiveness,
Shines saving Christ love from his eyes.

WE ARE BORN WANTING to control our world in ways that please us. As I've so often quoted, we want to "be as gods" (KJ Gen. 3:5). Which to me means that we actually don't want to *be* God or even be *like* God (as some translations say). But we do want to operate *as* a god, controlling our own personal little corner of the world.

And yet living in that small space can be very lonely. No other human being can actually know what's in our heart. And so it's easy to spend most of our natural lives running around in circles, willfully and desperately, trying to fill or satisfy the loneliness inside, loneliness that I had a lot of for a few years.

A few months after my saving moment experience, I was visiting my parents and thinking how nice it had been to spend a few days with other people in the house. I clearly recall opening the stairway door so I could run up and get my things to fly back to my solitary life in Boston. And then

I stood still in amazement at the clarity of this thought—Christ was right there with me and would always be there with me. I'd never be alone again.

Which is why I now say, we are all alone inside ourselves *until* we open ourselves to the Lord. The Saviour knows the lonely "me" that lives in consciousness, the part that no one can know. And it is in this unseen part of us where Christ's smile of comfort and forgiveness and healing happen. As Jesus says, "Those who love me will keep my word, and my Father will love them, and we will come to them and make our home with them" (NRSV John 14:23). His unseen and continuing companionship is the Lord's wonderful surprise.

16

Living larger, stronger, calmer
As we walk each hour with him
Feeds the spirit of believing,
A vibrant life too real to dim.

ALL DENOMINATIONS HAVE THEIR flaws. And the one I grew up with certainly had some. But it did open my heart to an awareness of spiritual life. I've always known that who we are is more than what we see here. That could be why Lewis' reference to the Lord's "larger, stronger, quieter life" made sense to me as soon as I read it.

But we aren't the ones who can extend the scope of our lives. We aren't the ones who can originate lasting strength. And we aren't the ones who can make a satisfying calm. As much as my earlier denominational believing would reject it, I'm now completely assured that this greater potential of life is what the Saviour brings to each of us. We live because he lives. As Jesus says in John, "The bread of God is the one who comes down from heaven and gives life to the world" (CEB 6:33).

Christ's life is as essential to us as bread, as the food we eat. It is Christ who sustains and nourishes our "spirit of believing." Whenever we start mingling our natural self-reliance and self-effort with our religious believing, we either lose our faith or sink it in a selfish quagmire of pride. That's because, as Jesus says, "The Spirit is the one who gives life and the flesh doesn't help at all" (CEB John 6:63).

Our helplessness in this whole process of faith and believing has grown to be a major source of comfort for me. So the only need for me and for you, day after day after day, is to practice intentional and deliberate relaxing back, placing every initiative in God's hands. When we do this, the Lord's vibrant life flows in—in just the way Lewis described in *Mere Christianity* ("Is Christianity Hard or Easy?").

Larger than …

Larger than ever-spreading sky,
Stronger than ev'ry law of earth,
Calmer than a mirror-like sea,
Is the God-Life that gives you birth.

Larger than any span of time,
Stronger far than bone and sinew,
Calmer than nature's ebbing flow,
Is the God-Love that breathes in you.

Living larger, stronger, calmer
Is what the Saviour comes to show
To his Father's loved and loving
Children who labor here below.

Larger than all our loneliness,
Stronger than all our willful cries,
Calmer with each new forgiveness,
Shines saving Christ love from his eyes.

Living larger, stronger, calmer
As we walk each hour with him
Feeds the spirit of believing,
A vibrant life too real to dim.

Patricia Hofer (2013)

17

Day by day the manna fell;
O to learn this lesson well!
Still by constant mercy fed,
Give me, Lord, my daily bread.

Josiah Conder (1836)

IN MY TWENTIES AND thirties, my life grew progressively more difficult. As I've written before, everything caught up with me. I was isolated in a large city following a failed marriage. The pain of abscessed teeth hounded me day and night. And my bills overpowered my money. But the harshest and most significant reality for me was that I was largely responsible for the mess I was in.

I'd always been someone who looked to the future. Hoping that things would get better was my way of soldiering through the present. And then, for the first time in my life, I didn't see a way forward. It would take years, if ever, to repair or rectify all that had gone wrong. Months of depression followed.

During that time, the words of this poem by Josiah Conder became a mainstay. My own faulty willfulness had finally forced me into living "day by day." And, as flawed as I was, the "constant mercy" of God that flowed from this poem sustained me and kept me going.

Christians are often tempted, as I was, by the idea that praying and following the rules can protect us from the pitfalls that others face. And yet, Jesus doesn't promise a trouble-free life. "Do not worry about tomorrow," he says, "Tomorrow will have its own worries. The troubles we have in a day are enough for one day" (NLT Matt. 6:34).

To be human is to have "troubles ... enough for one day." And yet, as miserable as the overall picture might appear, I discovered that small things can give this one day pleasant moments. Kindnesses, from others and to others, can warm our heart. Focusing on simple, present-day tasks can calm our spirit. And letting go, not relying on our own self-effort at all, washes away stress and burden. Inspired and sustained by Conder's poem, I still pray, "Give me, Lord, my daily bread."

18

"Day by day" the promise reads;
Daily strength for daily needs:
Cast foreboding fears away,
Take the manna of to-day.

Josiah Conder (1836)

THE WORD FOREBODING HAS to do with the future, our dread of what lies ahead. Such fears and worries don't necessarily have to be about big things. For example, when I first began teaching high school students five days a week, I was always filled with foreboding on Sundays. The idea of having to get up and go back to work on Monday destroyed whatever joy might be found. Eventually I did learn how to manage this routine dread of my job by telling myself, "Monday's not here yet. I don't have to think about it right now because it's not here yet."

But other "foreboding fears" aren't so easy to dismiss. Certainly some upcoming medical procedures haunt us with anxiety. Or we might be dreading weather, as in a tornado season. Perhaps we're fearing job loss or losing our home. These future fears, these unsettling possibilities, just hang out there, blocking the horizon, darkening our path forward.

The way I got through the time of my divorce, and the way I still try to live my life, is by constantly reminding myself to stay within the day. How things will be tomorrow or next week or next year aren't mine to carry. God supplies the strength "daily" for the needs we encounter "daily." His is not a storeroom of piled up strength just in case we need it!

Certainly the disciples felt some "foreboding fears" over what was to come when Jesus left them. And yet he told them, "But make up your mind not to worry beforehand how you will defend yourselves." The same Lord who was walking and talking with them in that present moment was still going to be there when they needed him, supporting each one of them with "words" and "wisdom" (NIV Luke 21:14-15). I've always felt this to be a comforting promise for each of us as well.

19

Lord, my times are in Thy hand;
All my sanguine hopes have planned
To Thy wisdom I resign,
And would make Thy purpose mine.

Josiah Conder (1836)

"SANGUINE HOPES," those cheerful, wishful things that we look forward to, are just the opposite of the "foreboding fears" in Conder's previous stanza. But this kind of wishful thinking can be just as big a stumbling block. In the first part of our lives, it is easier to expect that our happy and often ambitious plans will really happen. But that kind of optimism gets harder and harder after we've experienced some of life's reversals.

The children of Israel, for example, grumbled that their journey after leaving the slavery of Egypt wasn't what they'd planned or expected. And so they looked back, wistfully recalling that time when they "ate bread to the full" (Ex. 16:1-3). The problem with "sanguine hopes" is that they not only focus our attention on the desirable things we want to have happen but also on the things we wish we could return to. Both behaviors keep us from focusing on the present moment.

What kept the Israelites persevering for the next forty years, however, could not have been based in that kind of wistfulness. Wishful thinking doesn't push back despair. And the yearning that looks backward doesn't show us the way forward. That's why the daily "manna" that Moses promised the Israelites had to have been more than just the expectation of something to eat. They were also learning to trust, to abandon control and allow God to hold their future.

The kind of hope that comes with this surrender is indeed anchored in the eternal. And yet it must begin right here and right now. It must be practiced and nourished day by day in moments of humility and yielding. How effortless and sustaining faith can be when we finally let go and say, "Lord, my times are in Thy hand." I love those words!

20

Thou my daily task shalt give;
Day by day to Thee I live;
So shall added years fulfil,
Not my own, my Father's will.

Josiah Conder (1836)

IF THIS WERE THE last day on your job or the last day in your current home or the last day with a loved one, how would you live it? What would you notice or appreciate within each minute and each hour? Learning to live deliberately with God, to make our time with the Lord as important as these other significant experiences, is our "daily task."

That's because, as Brother Lawrence discovered, each minute in our lives is an opportunity to open our hearts to God's "abiding Presence." Wherever he went and during whatever menial task he was assigned, Brother Lawrence tried to maintain "an habitual, silent, and secret conversation of the soul with God" (The Practice of the Presence of God, *xi*, 31).

I like to visualize God's "abiding Presence" as it appeared when the Lord's spirit blew through the room and blazed in people's hearts on the day of Pentecost. They were assured, right then, that Christ was still going to be with them, would always be sustaining and comforting them. And that same Spirit of the Lord is by your side and my side right now, walking with us and talking to us, wrapping his light and love around us. But, just as Brother Lawrence realized in the 17th century, living in these right-now moments with a heart open to God takes practice.

I've found it helpful to pause before I race out to meet the day, to fall back and sit quietly and thoughtfully for a while. It's kind of like offering an invitation, really, a way of saying, "Lord, this day, this moment, is yours." Finding the time to live as Brother Lawrence described, living for God and in God and with God, is a daily challenge. And yet, when we open ourselves to these inspired moments, the whole direction of our life changes.

Day by day the manna fell;
O to learn this lesson well!
Still by constant mercy fed,
Give me, Lord, my daily bread.

"Day by day" the promise reads;
Daily strength for daily needs:
Cast foreboding fears away,
Take the manna of to-day.

Lord, my times are in Thy hand;
All my sanguine hopes have planned
To Thy wisdom I resign,
And would make Thy purpose mine.

Thou my daily task shalt give;
Day by day to Thee I live;
So shall added years fulfil,
Not my own, my Father's will.
Amen.

Josiah Conder (1836)

21

Dear Lord, make me better,
Better at being me.
Lift my soul to innocence,
From self and greed make free.

DURING THE EARLY PART of my life, I wasn't very good at being me. No one could be any more vulnerable and at the same time more assertive than I was. In public I pushed in because I was desperate for validation, and then in private I rolled up into a ball of insecurities. By the time I reached my 30's, I didn't like "me" at all.

My feelings of self-worth were trampled. Any self-satisfaction I might have harbored became lost in moments of humiliation. And finally, I was forced to abandon the most difficult "self" of all (at least for me), self-effort. My absolute inability to fix or manage my life made me ready for the Lord's regeneration.

After my saving moment, I found a very helpful analogy for this improvement process in Lewis' *Mere Christianity* chapter, "Counting the Cost." He sees human hearts as similar to houses that need renovation. When we allow it, Lewis wrote, God will change our heart—he will remodel or "rebuild that house." The challenge for us, however, is that the Lord will start "knocking the house about in a way that hurts abominably and does not seem to make sense." And then, according to Lewis, the Lord will surprise us by "building quite a different house" from the one we expected or planned for!

What Lewis doesn't say here is that this new "house" is what makes us better at being who we are. That's because the uniqueness of heart that the Lord has in mind for each one of us contains a fuller individuality and a more fulfilling life. Who we are "in Christ" is not only better—it is who God always intended us to be.

22

Free my heart from bearing
The things that bring me shame,
Regrets that keep me wakeful,
More doubts than I dare name.

THIS VERSE DESCRIBES THE real challenge in the Lord's remodeling project, our stubborn resistance. I wasn't very successful at making my young life work. But I just kept willfully pushing forward. During this time of self-reliance, even small accomplishments were immediately followed by regret or embarrassment, the insecurity that I should have done things differently. I was surely laboring "in vain" to "build the house" (Ps. 127:1).

Whenever my Christian believing suggested that I surrender to some kind of regeneration, I'd "prayerfully" determine what I thought needed remodeling and then ask the Lord for *his* help while I worked on *my* project. Then one day, after some particularly difficult and disastrous weeks, I surprised myself (and probably the Lord as well). I gave up. I was never going to regenerate myself into being more charitable and kind, and my heart reached out with the plea, "Please Lord, teach me to love."

Well, *katy bar the door*, as the old saying goes. Apparently I was finally humble enough and sincere enough to open myself to the Lord's renovation plans. Some "walls," ones that I actually hoped to keep, are no longer there. And some "additions," likely not even visible on the outside, have caused dramatic course changes in my heart. That's why none of us can tell from the outside, and therefore shouldn't judge, where another person is in Christ's regeneration project.

What I do know is that the Lord walked in and freed my heart in a unique way. He revealed a more peaceful and more loving person there than I could ever have imagined. And the wonder of it is that Christ has this very individual, special kind of uniqueness planned for each of us. Are you ready for it?

23

**Name again the virtues
That God does give to all.
Bring to my mind the goodness,
My better deeds recall.**

OUR LOVING FATHER AND Creator breathed His spirit of goodness into every human heart. As Paul wrote, not just to those at Philippi but to all of us: "God is the one who enables you both to want and to actually live out his good purposes" (CEB Phil. 2:13). Opening ourselves to this goodness, to what is truly "purity of heart," is what separates us from the world's natural selfishness.

That said, when worldly self-interest masquerades as goodness, I easily get fooled. One very tempting example for me is pride—a quality that, according to Lewis, "leads to every other vice." As much as we recognize pride in others, wrote Lewis, we are usually "unconscious" of it in ourselves. That's why pride can "smuggle itself into the very centre of our religious life" (*Mere Christianity*, "The Great Sin").

The tricky part for me, and perhaps for everyone, is that the world justifies and encourages our competitiveness and assertiveness—even considers them to be "virtues." But

God expects more of religious believing than the self-focus and aggressiveness of the natural world. And one of Jesus' parables shows us clearly what that expectation is. During prayer, we see a Pharisee, standing proudly, exalting himself, saying, "God, I thank you that I am not like other people." And then we turn and see a tax collector, standing humbly "at a distance," looking down at his feet saying, "God, have mercy on me, a sinner" (NIV Luke 18:10-14).

The spirit of Christ's humility and goodness is always present in every human heart. But, for this "more" of who we are to shine forth, for it to warm our souls and those of the people we meet, we must allow ourselves to be less.

24

Recall, too, simple truths,
The ones you know I love,
Sweet bits of inspiration
That filter from above.

FOR ME, THE SIMPLEST, most inspiring truth is the wonder of Christ's presence. And the words of the second poem on St. Patrick's Breastplate assure me daily of that presence. That's why I've added the poem as an essential last page to this book.

In its simple, most basic way, this prayer asks Christ to be "with me" and "within me." I grew up with the idea that God was present everywhere, but I still felt pretty much on my own at times. My daily walk with the Lord has changed all of that. Rather than being passive or disinterested, Christ is always trying "to win" more and more of my heart and your heart—trying to draw each of us away from the selfish concerns of this world.

Then, too, I like feeling the Saviour's love and support "beside me." This happens most when I'm alone and quiet. But I've also been aware of Christ's nearness when I turn everything over to him while serving others. When I'm overwhelmed, I pray, "You do this, Lord, I can't." And amazing things happen. He reaches into people's hearts, comforting them and giving them joy.

Another simple and comforting thought from this prayer is that the Lord is "behind me" and "before me." I can let go of the burdens of the past and my dread of the future because Christ is now and always has been present with me. And, regardless of what I must face, the Lord's sheltering and protecting presence is "beneath me" and "above me" — "in quiet" and "in danger."

These lines attributed to St. Patrick assure us that we are not on a lonely pilgrimage. During illness or loss or abandonment, the Spirit of Jesus, the Living Saviour, is always present "to comfort and restore" us. Oh, the joy and simplicity of such truths!

25

Above the earth's dark clouds
That hover, oh, so near,
With natural wants and needs,
Not what my heart holds dear.

THE "WANTS AND NEEDS" of human beings usually show themselves in the ways we attempt to manage everything. We naturally want to keep a tight-fisted control on our money and on our health and physical wellbeing. But for Christians, and probably for most everyone else, the worst kind of managing shows itself in our relationships with other people.

For example, this kind of managing can operate under the disguise of "concern" or "kind advice" or "help." Our need to impose our will can also hide within the desire to organize or clean or coordinate—managing not only our own environment but everyone else's as well! Even timidity and false humility can become unwitting tools to manipulate others for our own purposes.

I find it interesting, for example, that Peter was actually trying to control Jesus (perhaps out of fear for his own dignity) when he said, "No, you shall never wash my feet"

(NIV John 13:8-9). And at another time when Jesus was predicting his crucifixion, Peter said, "Never Lord! This shall never happen to you." Jesus corrected Peter sharply, telling him that he did "not have in mind the concerns of God, but merely human concerns" (NIV Matt. 16:22-23). Things were going to change—no matter how much Peter didn't want that to happen.

And change is going to happen to us and to those around us. I had to fall flat on my face before I learned to let go, to release my hold on what I perceived my life to be and my "human concerns." And I'm still no expert at doing so. Now, however, when I'm struggling in relationships with others, I usually can more quickly abandon my intentions—what I think or what I want. "They're yours, Lord. You take them. And while you're at it, take me too."

26

Dear Lord, make me better,
Better than what I've been.
Help me to feel thy favor,
Bless me over again.

HOWEVER ORIGINAL THEIR CLAIMS appear to be, underlying religions and philosophy and even psychology we find one basic idea: human beings are here to improve. The challenge, of course, is discovering what those improvements need to be and how those changes can become not only possible, but permanent.

What John and Charles Wesley discovered was that people might experience remarkable Christian conversions, but then, as time went by, they'd fall back into the struggle and burden of their lives. This led the Wesleys and others to embrace what they understood to be the Lord's "second blessing." It recognizes that, no matter how all encompassing and instantaneous a conversion is, the person God intends us to be emerges more gradually, as Christ's Spirit works its way in us, making holier lives.

That was certainly true for me. As I wrote in my first book, after my dramatic saving moment of conversion, at the end of that day, who I was in my life had not changed that much—only the burden and the aloneness were gone. Joy was once again possible. But many changes still needed to be made in my life. The Spirit's remodeling job of regeneration was and still is far from over for me.

That's what makes Christianity unique. Jesus Christ didn't just come two thousand years ago, demand our conversion, and then stand back to evaluate how well we do. The living Lord is beside each of us right now, inspiring our hearts, enabling kinder, gentler motives and making greater charity possible. When we let go of the person we are trying to make ourselves be, when we yield, who we are in Christ starts to emerge. "Through him" we become better than we could ever be alone. For me, that's the "second blessing."

Sanctifying Grace

Dear Lord, make me better,
Better at being me.
Lift my soul to innocence,
From self and greed make free.

Free my heart from bearing
The things that bring me shame,
Regrets that keep me wakeful,
More doubts than I dare name.

Name again the virtues
That God does give to all.
Bring to my mind the goodness,
My better deeds recall.

Recall, too, simple truths,
The ones you know I love,
Sweet bits of inspiration
That filter from above.

Above the earth's dark clouds
That hover, oh, so near,
With natural wants and needs,
Not what my heart holds dear.

Dear Lord, make me better,
Better than what I've been.
Help me to feel thy favor,
Bless me over again.

Patricia Hofer (2011)

27

Dear Lord and Father of mankind,
Forgive our foolish ways!
Reclothe us in our rightful mind,
In purer lives Thy service find,
In deeper reverence, praise.

John Greenleaf Whittier (1872)

GOD KNOWS OUR "FOOLISH ways" and our prideful ways—
the selfish things we do and the grudges and hurts we often
carry around for far too long. But the "Lord and Father" of
humankind also knows our need for Him. He knows how
much we seek some comforting connection beyond ourselves. And, since childhood, the calming presence of Christ
that flows through this hymn has always touched me.

Originally, the words were part of an extended poem.
Whittier was rejecting what religious believers do, and
what they have always done—which is to rely too much on
external, physical worship as a way to connect them with
God. Being a Quaker, Whittier knew that it was the "inward
light" of Christ that brings us comfort and draws us near.

The mystery that first emerged with Jesus' resurrection,
the beautiful secret of Christianity, is that God the Father

never meant His children to walk through life alone. And He didn't intend the earthly trials we encounter here to be some kind of a pass or fail test. Instead, He sent Jesus Christ, the living Saviour, to be "God with us," always. His presence at our side is God's forgiveness. His compassion is the saving love that cleanses our heart and purifies our intentions.

So we can stop relying so much on our "foolish ways," the desperate things we do to find God. He isn't hiding. He's always right here. We need only to open our hearts, to make room for Christ's warmth and vibrancy and strength. And the best way to begin, as Whittier wrote, is with the meekness of listening, the stillness and humility of no words, the "deeper reverence" of "praise."

28

In simple trust like theirs who heard
Beside the Syrian sea
The gracious calling of the Lord,
Let us, like them, without a word
Rise up and follow Thee.

John Greenleaf Whittier (1872)

FOR MOST OF US, having trust probably doesn't appear to be so simple, particularly if by *simple* we mean *easy*. No one can show us how to trust. And perhaps worst of all, we believers don't always know for sure whether we're truly trusting or just deceiving ourselves. But the Lord knows.

For example, Jesus wasn't throwing out a blind invitation to an unknown crowd "beside the Syrian sea." His attention was already focused on the willing and open hearts of Simon Peter and his brother Andrew, and James and John, two other brothers. At that moment, these men likely didn't even fully understood what Jesus meant by his promise that they would be "fishers of men" (Matt. 4:19; Mark 1:17). But they quit fishing anyway, and they walked away with Jesus. Such trust wasn't easy—they left everything behind. But it was singular, a "simple trust" in the Lord himself.

I've always visualized leaving everything behind in this way as similar to our letting go of a lakeside dock — knowing full well that we can't swim! All that we're sure of at that point is that we're done with the dock. And the "dock" that dominates our experience is our physical body and brain and the identity they give us. That's why death is so scary. No matter what we choose to hold onto — religious promises or reincarnation research or even well-documented "near death" experiences — that moment of letting go is a huge moment of trust.

For me, it's been easier to trust a Person rather than a theory or philosophy or doctrine. The living Saviour, who has guided and companioned me through many struggles, isn't ever going to abandon me. And that's true for you as well. The Lord knows each of us. His outreached hand is waiting, open and ready for ours.

29

Drop Thy still dews of quietness,
Till all our strivings cease;
Take from our souls the strain and stress,
And let our ordered lives confess
The beauty of Thy peace.

John Greenleaf Whittier (1872)

"STRAIN AND STRESS" AND "strivings" result from our natural need to survive. It's hard to imagine our life without them. I remember once, in frustration, smacking a large black widow spider with a fly swatter—several times I thought. But I didn't find any remains. Then, a couple of days later, I saw it sitting in its corner web, rather the worse for wear. But it was still striving!

Human beings have the same survival instinct as that spider. For us, however, it emerges as the determination to influence and control every least aspect of our lives. Our self-dependence and self-reliance, the need to manage our food and clothes and worldly knowledge, might actually be the original sin that the Genesis writer is describing (Gen. 3).

This desire to control everything requires that we be sovereign in our own particular corner of the world. And yet Jesus tells us we are to yield to God's sovereignty. As much as we might think otherwise, Jesus tells us that the "body," (a Greek word that can mean the wholeness of who we really are), is "more than clothes" and "more than food" (Matt. 6:25-33). Of course these things are important. But the wholeness of our relationship with God is the most important.

The reality is that the world is going to roll on without us, without our imagined sense that we are controlling it—without our demands and our opinions and our concerns. Falling back from all the pushing and shoving, yielding just for a moment, allows the Lord to order our day, to take the burden from our shoulders and move it onto his. How effortless the "dews" of his quietness and the "beauty" of his peace!

30

Breathe through the heats of our desire
Thy coolness and Thy balm;
Let sense be dumb, let flesh retire;
Speak through the earthquake, wind, and fire,
O still, small voice of calm.

John Greenleaf Whittier (1872)

ONE OF MY FAVORITE accounts in the Old Testament is about Elijah. He had gotten carried away in his jealous defense of God's covenant and had been forced to flee for his life to escape Jezebel. Finally, in utter self-abandonment, he sat under a tree in the wilderness and asked to die. "I have had enough, Lord," he said. "Take my life; I am no better than my ancestors" (NIV 1 Kings 19:1-12). Such despair. Such well-earned guilt.

But God didn't give up on Elijah. He sent an angel to bring him to Horeb, "the mountain of God." After Elijah confessed his guilt again, he was called to "Go out and stand on the mountain in the presence of the Lord, for the Lord is about to pass by."

First, "a great and powerful wind tore the mountains apart and shattered the rocks." Then there was an earthquake, and then a fire. In antiquity, earth, water, air, and fire were the four basic elements of nature. But, says the Old Testament, "the Lord was not in" these.

His Presence came, instead, as "a still small voice" or "gentle whisper." Elijah, who had killed other prophets in "the heats of [his] desire," Elijah, who had fled in fear when he thought his own life would be taken. That same Elijah experienced the cooling balm of the Lord's forgiveness and blessing.

It's comforting to know that the Lord isn't going to give up on us, you or me. Through all the turmoil in our lives, the clamor of nature and the roar of our sensuality and selfishness, God breathes into us, into each human heart, the gentle whisper "of calm."

Dear Lord and Father of mankind,
Forgive our foolish ways!
Reclothe us in our rightful mind,
In purer lives Thy service find,
In deeper reverence, praise.

In simple trust like theirs who heard
Beside the Syrian sea
The gracious calling of the Lord,
Let us, like them, without a word
Rise up and follow Thee.

Drop Thy still dews of quietness,
Till all our strivings cease;
Take from our souls the strain and stress,
And let our ordered lives confess
The beauty of Thy peace.

Breathe through the heats of our desire
Thy coolness and Thy balm;
Let sense be dumb, let flesh retire;
Speak through the earthquake, wind, and fire,
O still, small voice of calm.

John Greenleaf Whittier (1872)

31

Christit, whose glory fills the skies,
Christ, the true, the only Light,
Sun of Righteousness, arise,
Triumph o'er the shades of night;
Dayspring from on high, be near;
Day-star, in my heart appear.

Charles Wesley (1779)

THE VERSES OF THIS Charles Wesley hymn contain some of the first glimmers of Christ-light that stirred my heart. Because the words were in the hymnal I grew up with, they were not unfamiliar. But after my conversion experience, they resonated with me and moved me in a very different way. Whenever I see the first pinks and oranges of the morning sunrise, I think of this hymn.

Then I watch as Christ's brightness and beauty "fill the skies"—in the same way that his "true" and "only light" is always filling my heart. The Lord is always present, always triumphing over the "the shades of night," the many fears that roll over all of us in our sometimes precarious and often undependable lives.

Wesley is probably also referring to the "day star" or

"morning star" that we read about in 2 Peter. As it says there, the Lord "rises" in our hearts like "a light shining in a dark place" (NIV 2 Peter 1:19). Christ's light pushes back the darkness of loss and loneliness, opening our consciousness to his bright shining glory.

But the light of the Lord's presence isn't just within us. Wesley says it is a "day spring" that is always near us. If we think of Christ only as shining in our hearts, we might think we're left to confront the world alone. But the living Saviour is truly walking and standing right beside us. He knows our need and our uncertainty. He knows what is tempting us and what is scaring us. The Lord "from on high" is always "near," comforting and sustaining our continuing life.

32

Dark and cheerless is the morn
Unaccompanied by Thee;
Joyless is the day's return
Till Thy mercy's beams I see;
Till they inward light impart,
Glad my eyes, and warm my heart.

Charles Wesley (1740)

THE WORD UNACCOMPANIED APPEARS in most versions of
Wesley's second verse. But I did discover an older version
of the hymn decades ago where the word *unaccompanied* is
replaced with *uncompanioned*. How wonderful and needed
that friendlier image was to me at the time. My moments of
conversion had been preceded by months of depression and
feelings of abandonment. There was no joy in my heart.

But the Lord's comforting companionship changed all of
that. Suddenly I would catch myself humming a melody or
laughing at a television show. My step got lighter. And each
morning, when the "dark" and the "cheerless" would try to
push in, the Lord himself was always there, imparting the
"inward light" that brought the gladness back to my eyes
and the warmth to my heart.

Recently, I was checking translations of a Bible verse for the adult Sunday school class at church. The King James Version of Jesus' words reads: "But the Comforter, which is the Holy Ghost, whom the Father will send in my name, he shall teach you all things, and bring all things to your remembrance, whatsoever I have said unto you" (John 14:26).

I've always liked the word *Comforter* better than the *Advocate* or *Helper* of other translations. Today, however, I found that the Common English Bible translated this same word as "Companion." And a little further research showed that the Greek word being translated does include the idea of "consoler." To be comfortless is to be alone and isolated. And so it is the comfort and consolation of a companion that our loving Lord gives us. I like that!

33

Visit then this soul of mine,
Pierce the gloom of sin and grief;
Fill me, Radiancy divine,
Scatter all my unbelief;
More and more Thyself display,
Shining to the perfect day.

Charles Wesley (1740)

THE LORD DOES VISIT US, as Wesley says. But we are rarely open to him. We're too busy relying on ourselves, trusting in what we know, pursuing what we are just sure our life should be.

That's why, when I go through the lines of this third verse, I usually substitute the word self-effort for "sin." More often than not, it is my failed efforts and my unfulfilled self-will that bring the gloom. And, in my experience, "grief" has a lot to do with self-dependence. Right behind our mourning for loss lays the fear-filled question, "How will I manage alone?" Or, "How will I manage without my job"—or my house or my friends?

But the Lord's "Radiancy" can and does "pierce" through these moments of sadness and pride-filled managing. And

Christ, always the Counselor and Consoler, does "scatter" the doubts and distrust of our "unbelief" as well.

I remember one day, particularly, when this happened to me. Riding the train to work was often the best time of the day while I was living in Boston. One morning, I started worrying that maybe I was getting depressed again. Doubts were pounding at the door. Maybe my newly-found joy wasn't permanent. What would I do? What could I do?

But then, as I began going through the comforting images from Wesley's wonderful hymn, the train rolled by an outcropping of rock and bushes. As I looked up, one lone branch lit up my window. It was covered with beautiful fall leaves, dancing in the morning sunlight. The gloom was gone instantly. I can still see it decades later. In my heart, it is still "shining to the perfect day." Thank you, Charles Wesley.

Christ, whose glory fills the skies,
Christ, the true, the only Light,
Sun of Righteousness, arise,
Triumph o'er the shades of night;
Dayspring from on high, be near;
Day-star, in my heart appear.

Dark and cheerless is the morn
Unaccompanied by Thee;
Joyless is the day's return
Till Thy mercy's beams I see;
Till they inward light impart,
Glad my eyes, and warm my heart.

Visit then this soul of mine,
Pierce the gloom of sin and grief;
Fill me, Radiancy divine,
Scatter all my unbelief;
More and more Thyself display,
Shining to the perfect day.

Charles Wesley (1740)

34

I wonder what I would be
If God did not live in me.
Would I dream? Would I wonder?
Would I even hope to own
A soul through eternity?

AFTER DESCRIBING THE SIZE and magnificence of the night sky,
the psalmist asks the Creator: "What are human beings that
you think about them; what are human beings that you pay
attention to them?" (CEB Ps. 8:4). I love it that such questions were asked thousands of years ago. They indicate that
we humans have always introspected about who we are and
why we are and what we are.

We wonder about so many things. We review the past
and dream of a future. We imagine how we would like things
to be and get anxious about how they might instead be. And,
more importantly, we feel within ourselves something that
is unique, an individuality that is separate from everything
around us.

When God breathed His divine inspiration, his "breath
of life," into each living soul, He made our lives more than
just physical existence, more than just an endless stream of

sensations. He set us on an irreversible forward progress of experience. He inspired us with the higher capacities of insight and wondering and worshipping. Without these higher realms of consciousness, we wouldn't be able to know God. And He wants us to know Him. He created us to know Him.

For me, the psalmist is determining that as well when he says that God has made human beings "only slightly less than divine, crowning them with glory and grandeur" (8:5). Each of us is unique, each of us is God's special creation. Our consciousness, the part of us that questions and wonders and dreams, is the Creator's gift to every individual for all eternity. Opening our lives just a little to this inheritance, this "glory and grandeur," frees us and fills our soul with light.

35

Wouldn't I wander off in fear,
Seeking always, far and near,
Pushing and shoving my way
Along, without a purpose,
Nothing that rings true and clear?

WHAT CHALLENGES HUMAN BEINGS immediately is that we are born, fortunately or unfortunately, with little real understanding of who we were created to be. We might get glimmers here and there of something greater than this present life. But mostly we tend to follow the paths of others, competing and scrambling, finding ways to hold close what is ours.

We hear, and generally accept, that we live in a "dog eat dog world" where "the early bird catches the worm." Human beings also behave, at times, like "fraidy cats." And we are usually aware when we're craftily weaving "tangled webs" of deception and selfishness. At some point, though, each of us slams into the wall of the very natural existence that we've so willingly embraced—we're leveled by its unfairness and unconcerned randomness.

When this happens, we all have our own stories to tell—of

poverty or failing health, dissatisfaction or disappointment or loss. You know yours; I know mine. What we eventually discover is that operating as frail, isolated creatures, scurrying around on the surface of a planet makes less and less sense to us.

And so we begin asking questions and looking for answers. When that happens, God has us where He intends us to be. If physical existence were the Creator's only purpose for our presence here, we wouldn't be able to look up and beyond nature, to wonder what's "out there," to imagine the something "other" than what's here.

Even when we try to resist, when we attempt to argue ourselves out of the very things that our heart is telling us to embrace. Even when our thinking and believing get all confused or distorted. Even when we've lost our faith or never had it in the first place. Behind it all lies the Creator's grand intention—the growing and nurturing of our "living soul" for eternity.

36

I wonder what I would be
Without Christ alive in me,
Without his way of seeing,
Without his loving, unique
Individuality.

I SPENT THE FIRST half of my life believing that Christ was not Person but Principle, that Jesus was a Way-shower but not a Way-helper. My life became lonelier and lonelier and hugely burdened. So I don't need to wonder what it would be like "without Christ," without the companionship of the Lord. I've experienced it.

When I first began looking for a way out of my despair (although I wouldn't have recognized it as that at the time), I was drawn to a denominational poem called "Teach Me to Love" (Louise Hovnanian, 1908). In so many ways, this poem put my struggle and my yearning into words. "O Saviour," it prayed, "Help me to feel…Help me to seek."

Another pivotal moment occurred in a commuter train station. I was talking to a new friend who had been raised within the same denominational believing I was. But I blurted out anyway, "You know, I've come to the conclusion that there is more to Christ than we have learned." Her response surprised me. Her eyes lit up, and she said, "Exactly."

Regardless of where we are or of what we embrace or believe, the Saviour will find ways to reach us, now or later than now. Although the changes in me didn't seem very significant at any given point, I was gradually being drawn to the personhood of Christ, the living Lord who walks by my side and who moves the heavy burden from my shoulder to his.

The dramatic encounter that eventually happened was not a culmination of my search but rather a beginning—the beginning of a vibrant life filled with the daily company and comfort of my Saviour and Friend. What I've come to realize is that the unique individuality of each human being finds its full expression in Christ, who is himself a unique individual—and Lord of all.

37

With his star not in my soul,
What would make my being whole?
I'd not know and I'd not care
As I lived alone, apart,
That there was no higher goal.

ODDLY ENOUGH, PART OF me has always liked living "alone, apart." Because I was five and six years younger than my sister and brother, I played by myself most of the time. Then, too, I'm just naturally an introvert, someone who is actually energized by time alone. That said, eventually the despair that comes with isolation closes in on we humans, whether we're introverted or extroverted.

As the Genesis writer wrote, God didn't create us to "be alone" (Gen. 2:18). Relationships are the single most important theme in the Old Testament—interactions between God and prophets, between family members, and between differing ethnic believers. And in the New Testament, Jesus' three-year mission began with his calling disciples, friends to walk with him, willing hearts that would learn from him—followers that would go out into the world and speak for him.

Clearly, God's intention is for us to communicate and

share with each other. When the living spirit in our hearts encounters the living spirit in the hearts of others, we gain a fuller understanding of ourselves—and of Him! We become less self-centered, kinder. This might seem obvious to most of you. But it wasn't all that clear to me at earlier stages in my Christian experience. During those times, I rather enjoyed being an "ivory tower" Christian, not all that much into knowing others or helping them.

But then, after my conversion encounter, the Lord changed that. He started nudging me, pushing me out to help those in need. To become active in a church. To share my Christian walk in my writing. As I became more open to others, talking with them and discovering ways to help and comfort them, the Lord began dropping new friends across my path—not only the ones who needed me but the ones I needed! What a lovely "higher goal."

38

God be praised! That is not me,
Never what He meant to be
On that bright and shining day
When He breathed His breath of life
Into all humanity.

EVA WAS THE FIRST person the Lord dropped by for me to know. I walked out to my car one day, and there she stood in her flimsy slippers and old, soiled house dress. She had walked across the street to ask me for a ride to a nearby store.

My first thought was the hesitancy I was raised with—the fear she would start asking too much of me when it wasn't convenient. And I didn't have all that much money myself. But, rather than making an excuse as I would have in the past, I was obedient. I said, "Yes." I now know that the Saviour was standing there that day and that it had taken eight years of hungering and repentance and regeneration to open my heart to this request.

My time with Eva went on for several years. I won't say that I always loved her, or sometimes even liked her that much. But, we talked and laughed together. After having lost everything myself and after reaching the stage of not liking myself at all, it became easier and easier to be friends with her, to have compassion for her and for others, to judge them less and appreciate them more.

The yielding to the Saviour that occurred that day with Eva, that obedience, has sprouted into a vital and living walk of faith. I now know that the Lord marks out an individual, special path for each of us. Whenever selfish inclinations emerge that would keep me from helping others or that would make excuses for my not doing so, I remind myself that the Saviour is what they need, and my only job is to make room for his love in my heart.

39

Then, lest we forget what's done,
He sends Christ, His blessed Son.
Day by day he shines the way
Straight into our Father's heart,
Hope and home for everyone.

WHEN GOD, THE CREATOR, breathed His "living spirit" into the first human being, did He already know that each of us—every human being—would need His help? I think so. God understood the limitations we are dealing with and never intended to abandon us to them (John 3:16). So, as I see it, Christ was in the picture from the beginning. The Lord was always going to come to us, to remind us of who we are and to light "the way" forward.

But the time and place for Jesus' arrival had to be just right. The stability and peace of the Roman Empire was essential to establish roads and social structures. Trade routes to the East and busy centers of trade and culture all around the Mediterranean Sea broke down language barriers and allowed for the sharing of written laws and philosophy and learning.

But, that being true, the majority of the people still lived in a very limited world, one that offered them few opportunities and even fewer answers. Because lifespans were short and survival was a struggle, many hearts were open and ready for a savior, for some kind of salvation. And so, as Paul wrote, "...when the fullness of time had come, God sent his Son, born of a woman, born under the law" (NRSV Gal. 4:4).

We may not be able to control our motives or desires or selfish ways, but Christ can. We may not be able to free ourselves from the limitations of fear and insecurity. But the living Saviour can and does free us from these very things. His spirit is the "hope" that "shines" in each of our hearts. God intended always for His heart to be our "home."

40

**So we wonder and daydream
On our own immortal theme.
God's life hums within our soul,
And Christ's transforming glow
Makes us more than what we seem.**

IN ALL OF GOD's creation, we are the ones who "daydream." We can see hope and promise in rainbows and hum merrily an inspiring melody that comes from an arrangement of sounds. That's because we are the ones inspired by consciousness. Because of it, we can observe the rhythm of the seasons through the lens of logic. And we can appreciate that the sun's light is a spectrum of color and not just a bright glare.

Which reminds me of the small prism that a friend gave me. Hanging on its flimsy wire stand, it didn't look like much. But when I moved it into the garden window in my bedroom, it became alive. Each day it draws in the sunlight and splashes it as rainbows all over the walls and floors and furnishings!

And that is how Christ works in our lives. For most of us, understanding and relating to God, the Creator, isn't always that easy. For some, He seems unknowable, for others maybe aloof or distant, and worst of all even vengeful or angry.

But the Son, operating like a prism, shines God's divine light into our hearts and into our lives as a "transforming glow," a multitude of colors. The Lord's joy and intensity wash through consciousness, flooding us with vibrancy, pushing back at depression and debility. The Lord's strength radiates throughout our being, protecting us and sustaining us. And the Lord's love warms our heart, replacing fear and hatred with compassion and forgiveness.

The living Savior's presence separates out the marvelous "more" of our individuality, turning our reflections of the divine into eternal and unique signatures. All the beautiful colors of who we are come to us through Christ with his fuller, more abundant life (John 10:10).

More than what we seem

I wonder what I would be
If God did not live in me.
Would I dream? Would I wonder?
Would I even hope to own
A soul through eternity?

Wouldn't I wander off in fear,
Seeking always, far and near,
Pushing and shoving my way
Along, without a purpose,
Nothing that rings true and clear?

I wonder what I would be
Without Christ alive in me,
Without his way of seeing,
Without his loving, unique
Individuality.

With his star not in my soul,
What would make my being whole?
I'd not know and I'd not care
As I lived alone, apart,
That there was no higher goal.

God be praised! That is not me,
Never what He meant to be
On that bright and shining day
When He breathed His breath of life
Into all humanity.

Then, lest we forget what's done,
He sends Christ, His blessed Son.
Day by day he shines the way
Straight into our Father's heart,
Hope and home for everyone.

So we wonder and daydream
On our own immortal theme.
God's life hums within our soul,
And Christ's transforming glow
Makes us more than what we seem.

Patricia Hofer (2009)

41

Here, O my Lord, I see Thee face to face;
Here would I touch and handle things unseen;
Here grasp with firmer hand eternal grace,
And all my weariness upon Thee lean.

Horatius Bonar (1855)

HORATIUS BONAR, AN ORDAINED Scottish pastor, wrote hundreds of hymns. It was said that the hymns came to him during walks beside the ocean or along a brook. Or at other times he might be inspired by the rhythmic clatter of a train ride or the silent rhythm of the constellations shining above him.

And so, though Bonar does describe the Christian communion ritual in this hymn, he is also sharing something about the communion we have with the Lord at all times and in every place and part of our lives.

How do we see God "face to face" on a train ride as Bonar did, you might wonder. How do we see God when we're taking a walk or staring at the night sky? My answer is, wherever we are or whatever we're doing, the "open face" that sees and appreciates "the glory of the Lord" (KJV 2 Cor. 3:18) is our God-created consciousness.

This idea of connecting Christ to consciousness is not a new thing. Paul describes it as "the mind governed by the spirit" (NIV Rom. 8:6). And Christian mystics and contemplatives throughout the ages have often touched the hem of this inspired truth. For example, after writing that "God speaks face to face," St. Augustine explained that he was "speaking not of the face of the body but of that of the mind" (*Light from Light*, Dupré and Wiseman 74).

With this spirit of consciousness we can, as Bonar wrote, "touch and handle things unseen." The more room I make for Christ in my heart and mind in the morning, the more I'm able to "lean" on the Lord throughout the day, to abandon "my weariness." And that is a good thing.

42

This is the hour of banquet and of song;
This is the heavenly table spread for me;
Here let me feast, and feasting, still prolong
The hallowed hour of fellowship with Thee.

Horatius Bonar (1855)

BECAUSE I CAME LATE to the sacrament of communion, I walked up to the communion table for the first time filled with stage fright (a problem of mine) and embarrassment. Since then, I've continued to grow in appreciation for this public embrace of Christ that is so important for Christians. But I also still appreciate and love my separate, quiet moments shared with the Lord.

That's actually how the tradition of communion originated, with conversations between Jesus and his disciples while sharing a meal. And so, after the resurrection and ascension, early Christian groups followed the tradition, gathering in homes, sharing food and fellowship.

In 1st Corinthians, Paul established the symbols for this sharing when he wrote: "The cup of blessing which we bless, is it not the communion of the blood of Christ? The bread which we break, is it not the communion of the body of Christ" (KJ 10:16)? And the *Didache*, written late in the first century, formalized his words into the celebration of the Eucharist we have today.

And yet, to experience an intimate fellowship or rapport, and that is what communion means in English, we also need to embrace moments with the Saviour that come to us during all of our days. Such communion opens us to the spiritually unique person we were created to be, an individuality safely nurtured and filled with Christ's presence.

These singular, "hallowed" moments of fellowship with the Lord transform us. Instead of living our lives in lonely, self-dependent ways, we walk with Someone who is infinitely greater and stronger than we are. Communing with the Lord truly is a "heavenly table," one that is set for each one of us, each hour of every day.

43

Here would I feed upon the bread of God,
Here drink with Thee the royal wine of Heaven;
Here would I lay aside each earthly load,
Here taste afresh the calm of sin forgiven.

Horatius Bonar (1855)

AT ITS HIGHEST, COMMUNION with the Lord is a letting go, laying aside burdens and making room in our heart for him. Such yielding means that we place all aspects of our lives into his hands. At Gethsemane, Jesus modeled this self-abandonment for us when he said: "Father, if you are willing, remove this cup from me; yet, not my will but yours be done" (NRSV Luke 22:42).

Using this symbol of a cup at an earlier time, Jesus asked the sons of Zebedee, "Are you able to drink the cup that I am about to drink" (NRSV Matt. 20:22)? Viewed in this way, drinking "the cup" has become for me a metaphor for yielding, for obediently embracing whatever lies ahead. And so, sometimes during my morning quiet time with the Lord I think of the day ahead as "the cup."

It can become many things for me—some mundane, some very serious. For example, I might be thinking, "Dear Lord, if you are willing, remove this 'cup' of too many people and too many obligations." Or, "Dear Lord, if you are willing, remove me from this hot, drought-ridden state." At other times, the deliverance I need may be a desperately serious one, "Dear Lord, if you are willing, take away this 'cup' of my guilt" or "this 'cup' of pain and illness."

In those moments there is really nothing earthly or certain about the relief we're asking for, nothing natural or assured about the deliverance we hope to receive. Realizing that, we surrender anyway. We drink "the royal wine of Heaven." We abandon "each earthly load" and aspiration. We say, "not my will but yours be done."

44

Too soon we rise; the symbols disappear;
The feast, though not the love, is past and gone.
The bread and wine remove; but Thou art here,
Nearer than ever, still my Shield and Sun.

Horatius Bonar (1855)

WE WERE JUST IN Switzerland where we visited a small village church. Afterwards, a table was spread with the most wonderfully baked and delicious breads, of every kind and shape imaginable. Bread is so much a staple of human existence that today we even call it a comfort food!

Every meal Jesus shared with the disciples included bread. When he came to the two men on the road to Emmaus, "he was recognized by them in the breaking of the bread" (NASB Luke 24:35). And at the Sea of Galilee after the resurrection, the early morning meal he shared with them once more was fish and bread.

Although denominational believing may differ over the form of the body of Christ and the blood of Christ in the Eurcharist, for me there is only one focus—the Lord himself. We celebrate our nearness to the spirit of Jesus, the "bread of God," with the breaking and eating of bread.

That's because communion, for me, isn't ultimately about remembering someone who is gone as much as it is about celebrating someone who is always present. The living Saviour is always here with us, nearer than our heart, more who we are than our own soul—as basic to our very life as bread.

And I think that nearness is what Horatius Bonar is celebrating. We rise from the communion table, the daily one and the formal one, with the assurance that we are no longer isolated and self-dependent, but, instead, companioned and deeply loved. In spite of what we've done or will do, the Lord is still our "Shield and Sun"—our protection and our guiding light. Opening ourselves to that "nearer than ever" presence heals and sustains us. "The bread and wine remove; but Thou art here." Amen.

Here O my Lord

Here, O my Lord, I see Thee face to face;
Here would I touch and handle things unseen;
Here grasp with firmer hand eternal grace,
And all my weariness upon Thee lean.

This is the hour of banquet and of song;
This is the heavenly table spread for me;
Here let me feast, and feasting, still prolong
The hallowed hour of fellowship with Thee.

Here would I feed upon the bread of God,
Here drink with Thee the royal wine of Heaven;
Here would I lay aside each earthly load,
Here taste afresh the calm of sin forgiven.

Too soon we rise; the symbols disappear;
The feast, though not the love, is past and gone.
The bread and wine remove; but Thou art here,
Nearer than ever, still my Shield and Sun.

Horatius Bonar (1855)

45

Here see your hands,
Here wiggle your feet.
Here lies your heart,
Feel its every beat.

LONG BEFORE WE KNOW the importance of a beating heart, we look at our hands and practice using them. The same process works for our feet. Very quickly our hands and feet become natural extensions of who we are. They get us where we want to go and do what we want them to do—most of the time.

The problem, however, is that the natural world isn't fair at all in its distribution of physical talents. Just because we can move our hands or feet, for example, doesn't mean that they will continue to work as well or as long as we want them to. That variability and, perhaps, unreliability, applies to our heart as well. Sooner or later, through aging or disease, we're forced to confront the rather frail, limited nature of hands and feet and heart.

Then, like Job, we can't believe what's happened to us. We look to our friends for answers—or to our philosophy of life or our religious doctrines or our conventional wisdom.

Their answers don't satisfy us. Then, Elihu offers an answer to Job and us when he says, "But the spirit in a person, the Almighty's breath, gives understanding" (CEB Job 32:8). God is always speaking to us, says Elihu, but "no one perceives it" (33:14).

That's because, when we're physically strong and flourishing, it's easy to ignore "our living soul," the part of us that is inspired by God. And yet, the amazing thing is that this "spirit in a person" is not frail. This spirit of consciousness and understanding hums along in ageless and vibrant ways. In our minds we can climb mountains, dream daydreams, and, yes, talk with God.

And the truly lovely surprise is that there is nothing temporary at all about this uniquely inspired and ageless individual that God created us to be!

46

This is our life,
Appearing to be
All that we'll know,
All there is to "me."

WHAT APPEARS TO BE "me" but really isn't reminds me of an image I used in one of my earlier books. I described wheeling around a broad curve into a downhill straightaway on the mountainous road to Payson. In this race downhill, for just a few seconds, it appears as if the car is going to slam into the next mountain, landing on top of a huge junk pile of wrecked cars with other foolish drivers.

As silly as that sounds, this misperception is not unlike what our natural life appears to be now. As we speed through our days and years, blinded by everything except our physical existence, we start to imagine ourselves traveling full speed toward a brick wall called death. We see ourselves smashing into that wall, following all of humanity into oblivion, another kind of junk pile.

But God created each of us with a greater life than this "brick wall" inevitability. And He placed within us the capacity to see and appreciate that larger, stronger, calmer life—right here, right now. Opening ourselves to the spirit of Jesus, the Christ spirit in our heart, makes it possible for us to step back from this temporary, appearance of life. But first we must be willing to open our hands and let go.

We must abandon the self-interest and self-focus of what we proudly thought was our particular life. As Jesus tells us, "Whoever tries to preserve their life will lose it, but whoever loses their life will preserve it" (CEB Luke 17:33). As we change our perception of who we are, instead of seeing an impassable wall at the end of our years, we'll see our path continuing on. This frees us to live now in confidence, to be content and at peace. Comforted.

47

**But we are more
Than nature defines,
A living soul
With a conscious mind.**

MINDFULNESS HAS BECOME A popular practice once again. I say once again because such contemplation has likely been around as long as human beings have been around. What is truly new is that some modern neuroscience research now supports the idea that our brains and our "conscious mind" are two separate things.

For example, the brain is more or less pot-bound. Its neurons connect the various self-centered sensations and reactions and limitations of natural experience. The brain would keep me (and you) looking at where we put our feet, finding our next meal, and worrying about who or what is sneaking up on us!

Our consciousness, on the other hand, is the home of creativity, insight and intuition—the God-derived gifts that have propelled human beings forward. So it is the thoughtfulness that flows in from consciousness that needs to focus our mindfulness and our prayers.

That's because, when it comes to faith and religious believing, we need to recognize the brain as clearly and repeatedly a "false prophet." The writer of 1 John, a member of the community that followed the teaching of John the Apostle, warns early Christians that they must learn to recognize "false prophets." Followers were to "test the spirits to see whether they are from God" (NIV 4:1-2).

Similarly we need to "test" the thoughts that are governing our lives by tracing them back to their source. Christ-inspired thoughts are the ones that fill our hearts with love and peace, with enduring faith and healing consolation. The "more" that comes with a life "hidden with Christ in God" emerges as we consciously focus "on things above, not on earthly things" (NIV Col. 3:2-3).

48

Not here, not there,
But something apart.
"Lo, I'm with you,"
Speaking in our heart.

JESUS DESCRIBES THE KINGDOM of God like the smallness of a "mustard seed," like the transforming power of "leaven" or yeast, like a "pearl of great price" that we are to value above all else. And yet, these physical images or comparisons are the Lord's way of describing something that isn't physical at all, something wholly apart from the natural world we live in.

Jesus actually made this point to the Pharisees after they came to him asking about "when the kingdom of God should come." The kingdom of God, Jesus said, wasn't something they were going to see "with observation." They weren't going to be able to look at it and say, "Lo, here or, lo there!" Rather, says the Son of God, "the kingdom of God is within you" (KJV Luke 17:20-21).

This inner individuality, the Christ spirit in each heart, is God's gift to us in his "breath of life." It is now and will always be who we are. And the Lord himself will always be beside us, walking with us to guide and to comfort. Jesus assures us of that after his resurrection when he appeared to the disciples, saying, "All power is given unto me in heaven and in earth." As he sends them out to "teach all nations," the Lord reassures them, "Lo, I am with you always even unto the end of the world" (KJV Matt. 28:18-20).

Our conscious connection to God and His Christ is not limited at all by the physical nature of things. Wherever we are, whatever part of the world we're in or whatever part of the human timeline we're on, the living Saviour is always present and speaking to us. Once we realize this, once our minds and hearts become more available to him, we'll never feel alone again.

49

Giving comfort,
Pushing back the night.
Ever awake,
Lifting us to light.

WHEN WE'RE SICK OR scared or depressed, the darkness of night is often the worst time. That's what I experienced years ago when I had all the symptoms of a nervous breakdown. I couldn't eat or sleep, and because I couldn't relate to people, I shut myself away from family and friends. All I could think of during those weeks were my fears. I felt no joy, and I was terrified of the nights.

When I think of that time now, Jesus' promise about our being "full of light" comes to mind. I've always loved that. And yet Jesus says in the next sentence: "But if your eye is bad [or evil or unhealthy], your whole body will be full of darkness. If then the light that is in you is darkness, how great is the darkness" (NASB Matt. 6:22-23)!

Certainly my darkness was great. And though my fears back then may sometimes have swirled into the paranoia of being under siege, mostly it was the darkness of despair that pushed at me. My life had been filled with pressure and loss and loneliness. Like a drowning person trying to save myself, I thrashed around focusing only on what I needed to do and what I was failing to do. Filled with self-effort instead of self-surrender, I was desperately praying and pleading with God, hoping to pull His light down into my life

After about six weeks of turmoil, a turning point came around four o'clock one morning. I was shaking in bed after a sleepless night, terrified of something that I couldn't even identify or define. So I started singing hymns, verses that I now recognize were filled with Christ. He pushed back the darkness, filling my heart with his marvelous light. How comforting it is to know that the living Saviour is always awake, never for a moment leaving us alone in the dark of night.

50

A greater "me"
Than just hands and feet.
Christ's stronger heart,
An eternal beat.

IN MANY WAYS OUR body is like a car we happen to be driving.
It may be motoring us around right now but who we are is
greater than it is. And yet, we still allow this "car" of our
physical life to define us in limiting ways. Here we stand,
for example, the person with the flawed eyesight or the mal-
functioning heart. Or we might label ourselves as the person
with bad teeth or weak lungs or painful joints. The list of
bodily limitations and fears is endless.

What Jesus Christ does, what God sent him to do, is to lift
our gaze, to raise our eyes to see the person God intended
us to be, the one created in His image. As Jesus explains
to Nicodemus, "Whatever is born of the flesh is flesh, and
whatever is born of the Spirit is spirit" (CEB John 3:6).

To be "born of the flesh" is to believe we're defined by
the limited, genetic construction of our physical bodies. To
be "born of the Spirit" is to embrace the larger, more vibrant
consciousness of life that God is constantly creating in us.

And, if we thoughtfully look inside our heart, we'll realize that this greater individuality of who we are has always been there. We've always had a unique personhood, something separate from what the world sees.

Being "born anew," says Jesus, isn't something to be "surprised" about but something to gratefully embrace (3:7). To be "born again" or "born from above" is to abandon our dependence on physical impulse and instinctual function—to live "more abundantly" in the calm and quiet of Christ's eternity (KJ John 10:10). And the living Saviour is right here, always ready to help us do that. For me, that's what Christianity is about.

Our strength

Here see your hands,
Here wiggle your feet.
Here lies your heart,
Feel its every beat.

This is our life,
Appearing to be
All that we'll know,
All there is to "me."

But we are more
Than nature defines,
A living soul
With a conscious mind.

Not here, not there,
But something apart.
"Lo, I'm with you,"
Speaking in our heart.

Giving comfort,
Pushing back the night.
Ever awake,
Lifting us to light.

A greater "me"
Than just hands and feet.
Christ's stronger heart,
An eternal beat.

Patricia Hofer (2014)

51

Still, still with Thee, when purple morning breaketh,
When the bird waketh, and the shadows flee;
Fairer than morning, lovelier than daylight,
Dawns the sweet consciousness, I am with Thee.

Harriet Beecher Stowe (1855)

THIS MORNING ONCE AGAIN I sat in prayer looking out the east windows in my upstairs sitting room. I love the gray dark before dawn and the first gradual hint of pink or orange in the east. I love the waking birds and the fleeing shadows. And, of course, this is why I've always loved Harriet Beecher Stowe's inspiring poem.

The first time I greeted the morning reciting her lines is as clear to me as if it happened yesterday. My elbows were resting on the splintered weathering of the upstairs' windowsill while I looked past the familiar trees of our farm's front yard and on to the pink edge in the east. It's amazing, isn't it, how natural images and events, large and small, come and go. They clatter along in fast succession, like the movie frames from some rickety projector. And yet, once in a while, some gnat-like thought gently lights in our minds, framing an experience in eternity. And that's what happened to me that morning decades ago.

Since that inspiring moment as a young girl, the whispers of Stowe's lovely thoughts have followed me throughout my life. With her God-inspired words, the loveliness of the sunrise becomes a metaphor for the effortless and certain dawning of Christ in our heart.

And so this morning, I recited her verses, rejoicing in this gift of God's inspiring, the "sweet consciousness" of Christ's presence. And that presence is "fairer" and "lovelier" than all of the symbols for it that nature might provide. Each day, in the "still" stillness we hear the Lord whispering, "I am with Thee."

52

Alone with Thee, amid the mystic shadows,
The solemn hush of nature newly born;
Alone with Thee in breathless adoration,
In the calm dew and freshness of the morn.

Harriet Beecher Stowe (1855)

PERHAPS THE SUNRISE PLAYS a chord in the human soul because the sun's appearing is so beautifully out of our control, so effortless and certain for us—it just happens! Such passive involvement gives us peace.

While we humans tend to focus on tomorrow or next week or the coming years, nature's rhythms capture for us the "calm dew and freshness" of the moment, the newness of a single day lying before us. That could explain why Stowe herself had the habit of getting up at 4:30, walking and thinking in the freshness of the early morning.

And yet, as relaxing and inspiring as nature can be, Stowe's poem is also encouraging us to open ourselves to something more, to look up and away from the path at our feet. Nature may appear to be "newly born" each morning, but it opens its eyes with no sense of the past or wonder for the future. Natural things have no sense of themselves, no ability to step back and appreciate or evaluate. Only human consciousness has that.

But this conscious person that we are inside, this subjectivity that we have, might also make us uncertain sometimes. There's nothing simple about faith and rationality and self-knowledge. We can easily begin to think that we're carrying the burden of who we are all by ourselves. But we're not. The Creator's breath of life, the source of our consciousness, has never stopped flooding us with believing and connectedness. Once we open our hearts to Jesus Christ, we're always companioned. As Stowe rejoices, we're always "alone with Thee."

53

Still, still with Thee, as to each newborn morning,
A fresh and solemn splendor still is given,
So does this blessèd consciousness, awaking,
Breathe each day nearness unto Thee and Heaven.

Harriet Beecher Stowe (1812-1896)

The two Gospel descriptions of time with the Lord that I enjoy most are early morning ones. The first is described in Mark: "In the early morning, while it was still dark, Jesus got up, left the house, and went away to a secluded place, and was praying there" (NASB 1:35). I've always visualized him doing that, quietly slipping past the others to commune with his Father, to watch the first pink of sunrise.

The other morning time that I love to imagine is the one on the shore of the Sea of Galilee (John 21). It was early, at daybreak. Perhaps the water was quite calm, sloshing softly against the shore. The sun was rising and the resurrected Jesus was standing there, looking out across the lake.

Without the Lord walking with them, the disciples had decided to go back to fishing. They had to do something, they thought. And they were likely very despondent about it. Certainly, they had fished all night and hadn't yet caught anything. And then Jesus yells to them from shore, telling them to cast their net again "on the right side of the boat." And then, of course, it filled with fish. And they came ashore to share another breakfast with their living Lord.

I think Jesus is telling us to do that each morning as well—to cast our thinking "on the right side." Turning away from the limiting and worrying thoughts of nighttime, we open ourselves to the freshness of the Lord's new morning. His "nearness" pushes back the demands of the day. One by one by one we allow our hurts and worries and responsibilities to slide off of our shoulders. We can almost smell the fish sizzling on the coals. Thank you, Lord, for our breakfast feast.

54

When sinks the soul, subdued by toil, to slumber,
Its closing eye looks up to Thee in prayer;
Sweet the repose beneath the wings o'ershading,
But sweeter still to wake and find Thee there.

Harriet Beecher Stowe (1855)

WHEN I WAS A child, I heard this bedtime poem from my best girlfriend: "Now I lay me down to sleep. I pray the Lord, my soul to keep. If I should die before I wake, I pray he Lord my soul to take." All I got from this "prayer" at the time was the idea that I might die if I went to sleep! And that could be why I have always found Stowe's comforting verse about slumber so reassuring.

I have at times wondered, though, why Stowe used the singular "eye" instead of eyes. But now, after some thought and continued study, I think she might have drawn her description of the soul's "eye" from something that Jesus referred to. Before warning against trying to serve "two masters," he said, "The light of the body is the eye: if therefore thine eye be single, thy whole body shall be full of light" (KJ Matt. 6:22).

More recent translations of this verse replace *single* with words like *sound* or *clear*. But the Greek word that the KJV translated as *single* does contain a clear sense of union, a folding together. So, in a sense, when we slumber, our soul is single, a "closing eye," folding back into the light of Christ.

Many a night, when I'm tired and "subdued by toil," I consciously fold myself into the Lord's reassuring presence. He sustains and protects our soul, our conscious individuality, even when we're sleeping. So, whether we wake up here in our bedroom or in the next room of continuing life, we can rest comfortably saying: "Oh, Lord, 'keep' my soul, nurture and shelter it until I'm once again awake, once again finding you with me."

55

So shall it be at last, in that bright morning,
When the soul waketh and life's shadows flee;
O in that hour, fairer than daylight dawning,
Shall rise the glorious thought, I am with Thee.

Harriet Beecher Stowe (1855)

MORE AND MORE I'M comforted with the understanding that dying is really just another awakening, a continuing of our conscious life. The experience is probably like something that happens to us in childhood—when we fall asleep in one room only to wake up in the morning in another, not remembering how we got there or who carried us.

And we also can be reassured by what the disciples experienced on the day of Pentecost (Acts 2:1). Trusting wasn't any easier for them than it is for us. They lost their trust at the crucifixion, only to get it back in the resurrection. But then the Lord ascended, and, because they couldn't see him any more, they probably started to doubt and distrust what their own eyes had seen.

But this time they trusted enough to be obedient. They went to the Temple in Jerusalem and waited, just as the resurrected Jesus told them to do. Early Christians gathered in the morning to worship, and so I think this gathering was probably in the morning as well. And then the spirit of Jesus, the Holy Spirit, came again to stir their hearts, this time in a way that sustained them throughout their lives.

And we're never going to be abandoned either, never left to go it alone here or hereafter. When "life's shadows flee," we'll awake to encounter another bright morning, one "fairer than daylight dawning," just as Stowe described it. In a flood of love and inspiration, we'll awake to our continuing consciousness, our "living soul" (Gen. 2:7). God's tender presence and love will "still, still" surround us. We'll say then as we say now, "I am with Thee."

Still, still with Thee, when purple morning breaketh,
When the bird waketh, and the shadows flee;
Fairer than morning, lovelier than daylight,
Dawns the sweet consciousness, I am with Thee.

Alone with Thee, amid the mystic shadows,
The solemn hush of nature newly born;
Alone with Thee in breathless adoration,
In the calm dew and freshness of the morn.

Still, still with Thee, as to each newborn morning,
A fresh and solemn splendor still is given,
So does this blessèd consciousness, awaking,
Breathe each day nearness unto Thee and Heaven.

When sinks the soul, subdued by toil, to slumber,
Its closing eye looks up to Thee in prayer;
Sweet the repose beneath the wings o'ershading,
 But sweeter still to wake and find Thee there.

So shall it be at last, in that bright morning,
When the soul waketh and life's shadows flee;
O in that hour, fairer than daylight dawning,
Shall rise the glorious thought, I am with Thee.

Harriet Beecher Stowe (1855)

56

Please, Lord,
Hold me in this calm, secret place,
Confident, quiet, and free.
Circled around by your embrace
Where there's only you and me.

Not long after my life-changing conversion experience, I attended a Christmas Eve service with my sister and her family in a different denomination. The pastor referred to Christ before us, Christ beside us, and Christ within us. That was the first time that I'd heard the Lord described that way. And yet I immediately thought, "of course."

The Christ *before* me was easily appreciated. I'd always trusted and looked to God, the Father. Trusting and looking to the Son in the same way was effortless. And opening myself to Christ's presence *within* us was also easy to accept. As Paul wrote, we gain strength "through his Spirit in the inner man" or "inner being" (Eph. 3:16).

What I remember most clearly, though, after a lifetime of lonely struggle and self-effort, was the comfort of Christ *beside* me. Being "circled around" by the Lord's presence means that I, and you, are never isolated or alone. Now when

I'm feeling uncertain, I pause and let the Lord walk into the room ahead of me. When I'm facing something scary, I fall back saying, "Here it is, Lord. You take it."

The Greek words for *secret* and *mystery* can refer to something hidden, unseen. The wonderful secret within Christian believing is that the spirit of Jesus, though unseen, is still always with us. This is the mystery that the resurrection and ascension make possible. Jesus said then and continues to say now, "Lo, I am with you always" (Matt. 28:20). Before us, within us, and beside us—all around us in all times and in all ways.

57

Please, Lord,
Cleanse my sad heart with your spirit;
Light it, fill it with your peace.
So when you speak, I can hear it—
Selfish distractions all cease.

"GOD KNOWS YOUR HEARTS," Jesus says (Luke 16:15). The Father knows the person inside, the one we really are. And so, when Jesus refers to our "heart" in his teaching, the Lord is appealing to and talking to our inside conscious self.

He tells the Pharisees, for example, that they should focus less on "the outside of the cup and of the platter" and "cleanse first that which is within" (KJV Matt. 23:25-26). And in another place he says, that impurity or purity "come from the heart" (Matt. 15:18). It is there that the angry words and self-centered actions and destructive distractions originate. It is there that change and regeneration must occur.

And we Christians know this—most of the time. But, what we also have learned is that focusing on the "doing" of Christianity, putting on the outside garb of being a good Christian, is far easier for us than changing the intentions of our heart. Learning to love more and judge less is a heart change (Luke 6:37). Not storing up "treasures on earth" requires another heart change (Matt. 6:19). Meekness and mercy, purity of heart and peacemaking—these are heart changes (5:1-10). And there's nothing easy in the gradual, transformational demand that these beatitudes contain.

Which is why it is so important to realize that Christ also lives in our heart. His is the Spirit that can govern what we do and what we think. His is the light that floods and cleanses our heart, pushing out the selfish clutter that the natural life builds up. When we get out of the way, when we surrender, the Lord makes us better at being who we truly are. Jesus yielded to his Father when he said, "I can do nothing on my own" (NRSV John 5:30). And that is true for us as well.

58

Please, Lord,
Free my weary soul from worry,
Help me feel you by my side.
Shelter me from stress and hurry,
Loving Saviour, strength and guide.

As MUCH AS WE might start out with the idea that our parents know what we're thinking, we soon learn that they really don't. And it also isn't long before we realize that who we really are inside and what we really think is unknowable to others as well. That realization is an exhilarating thing—at first.

But eventually, this inner person starts developing and carrying inflexible biases and longstanding fears. Our soul becomes a hiding place for haunting regrets and favorite grudges and stubborn doubts. At least, those were the burdens that were wearing me down at a pivotal time in my life. I needed to own up to my failed marriage. Poverty and ill health made my pride and pretension truly silly. And the religious believing that I'd trusted all my life was failing me. Everything that I'd wrapped tightly around me as "me" was lost. Or at least I thought it was.

What I learned, though, is that our "living soul," the consciousness that God inspired, isn't meant to be a static, rigid place. This eternal, hidden part of our individuality needs, instead, to be more like a living underground cavern, something that contains the flowing water of regeneration and change. And I think that is what Jesus was telling the Samaritan woman when he offered her the "living water" that "bubbles up into eternal life" (CEB John 4:10-14).

The Lord is the only one who knows what we are really thinking, the burden our soul is carrying around. And Christ's spirit of "living water" is always present there in our heart, always ready to cleanse, strengthen, and transform us. We just need to be thirsty enough, and lonely enough, to allow that to happen.

59

Please, Lord,
Relieve my mind from managing
The tasks I must or would do.
Turn stubborn will into yielding
To wonder that comes from you.

WHEN WE LEARN THAT something isn't going to be our responsibility or isn't going to be as bad as we thought it might be, we say, "That relieves my mind." But our mind doesn't stay relieved very long, at least mine never has. That's because we humans are born with the constant drive to control and manage things—our health, our friends and family, our money and career, and even our society and government. So our consciousness is a busy place!

Where we get into trouble, though, is when we try to manage, or think we can manage, our relationship with God. I did that. My denominational believing had encouraged me to rely on my own thinking—to control my life by controlling my thoughts. And so, the more difficult things got, the more stubborn and self-reliant I became. I finally had to learn that God wasn't going to give me the job just because I relentlessly asked Him to. And God wasn't going to change others for my purposes, no matter how much I studied and prayed about it. Eventually, after years of stubborn willfulness, I surrendered.

As Jesus says, "you must accept the kingdom of God as if you were a child" (NCV Luke 18:17). Small children know that there are many things beyond their control. But that's not true for adults. The more control we think we have, the more stubborn and egotistical we become. We can be knocked down, wobbling there on all fours, but still refusing to let go—still giving God advice.

What I now know is that the Lord is waiting in each of those willful moments of struggle, saying, "Come to me, all of you who are tired and have heavy loads, and I will give you rest" (NCV Matt. 11:28). Oh, the wonder and relief of yielding, of childlikeness!

60

Please, Lord,
Show me my eternal calling.
Pour it over me anew,
The grace that keeps me from falling,
The restful Spirit that's you.

WRITTEN VERSIONS OF THIS poem have been coming to me
for many years. And yet the one verse that has stayed pretty
much the same through all of my revisions is this one.
Imagine my surprise yesterday when I finally realized what
it was about!

I was on the telephone with my ninety-seven year old
mother who lives in an assisted living facility. She began
describing, with amazement and some embarrassment, how
the workers sat down on the floor to cut her toenails and
massage her feet. This was very humbling for my proud
mother. Their doing that reminded her of Jesus, she said,
when he washed the disciples' feet.

Washing and anointing feet with oil was a custom in
Jesus time, but it was also something done by a servant or a
helper. So Jesus shocked the disciples when he laid his robes
aside and wrapped a towel around his waist, as a servant

would do. When he was done, Jesus said, "I have given you an example: Just as I have done, you also must do" (CEB John 13:1-15).

Serving others is what leads us to abandon our pride and self-focus—our aspirations and pretensions. That's why the most restful and grace-filled life, for a Christian or anyone else, necessarily calls us to help others in kind and humble ways. Empathy and compassion, self-knowledge and self-abandonment, come to us with God's grace. They are our "eternal calling." When we're down on the floor or on our knees, we don't need to worry about "falling"! It's a restful place to be, comfortably humble, down there with the Lord.

61

Please, Lord,
Take this, my plea, as your token,
Refine it, make it be true.
A vow that cannot be broken,
A life lived always with you.

GOD DIDN'T CREATE US to be self-existent units, wandering alone on our own self-determined journey. God created us to be with Him and husbanded by Him. And Christ's metaphor of the "true vine" helps to describe the spiritual, eternal connection we all have. Jesus says, "I am the vine, you are the branches." A branch can't exist separate from the vine. Its purpose is, quite simply, to allow the Lord's fruit-filled life to flow through it.

The only role we can play, then, is to be a branch, to be an avenue for the fruits of His grace. But such passive participation, such utter surrender, isn't really our plan—just as it wasn't Adam and Eve's. It certainly isn't anything I'd have considered before my conversion experience.

The surprise for me since those inspired moments, however, is that yielding and self-surrender continue to open me to the richest possible kind of experience—the kind where Christ's "larger, stronger, quieter life" flows into my heart (Mere Christianity 154). Instead of diminishing individuality, as we all so naturally fear, our openhearted surrender to Christ enlarges and strengthens who we are, filling our lives with a satisfying wholeness and a fulfilling peace.

This yielding is the life-changing perspective that I've been called to share in my Christian writing. My experience offers proof that the living Saviour is continually desiring and seeking a rich and inspiring connection with every human soul. Just before his crucifixion, Jesus prays, "Father, I want those you gave me to be with me where I am" (CEB John 17:24). The Lord wants you and me, each and all of us, to be with him. The calm and comfort of that reality is my witness to you.

Please, Lord,

Hold me in this calm, secret place,
Confident, quiet, and free.
Circled around by your embrace
Where there's only you and me.

Cleanse my sad heart with your spirit;
Light it, fill it with your peace.
So when you speak, I can hear it—
Selfish distractions all cease.

Free my weary soul from worry,
Help me feel you by my side.
Shelter me from stress and hurry,
Loving Saviour, strength and guide.

Relieve my mind from managing
The tasks I must or would do.
Turn stubborn will into yielding
To wonder that comes from you.

Show me my eternal calling.
Pour it over me anew,
The grace that keeps me from falling,
The restful Spirit that's you.

Take this, my plea, as your token,
Refine it, make it be true.
A vow that cannot be broken,
A life lived always with you.

Patricia Hofer (2015)

Christ be with me, Christ within me,
Christ behind me, Christ before me,
Christ beside me, Christ to win me,
Christ to comfort and restore me,
Christ beneath me, Christ above me,
Christ in quiet, Christ in danger,
Christ in hearts of all that love me,
Christ in mouth of friend and stranger.

❀ ❀ ❀

Discussed in chapter 24 and found at
http://prayerfoundation.org/
st_patricks_breastplate_prayer.htm

PATRICIA HOFER ENDED HER high school teaching career in the early 1980's and found her way to Boston for a job with a publisher. Besides learning to research and edit, she eventually had several articles published. After returning to Arizona, she taught freshman English and technical writing at Glendale Community College. Hofer is now retired and living in the lovely mountain town of Payson AZ. She continues learning and sharing in a wide variety of facebook groups and on her webpage www.yieldingtochristianity. com.

CPSIA information can be obtained at www.ICGtesting.com
Printed in the USA
LVOW08s1744100116

469984LV00002B/549/P